CW00822775

Building a relationship with important to me. I occasiona with details on new relea podcast news and the exclus my fans, such as exclusive Murder Tales Shorts and Freekly Oldacre novellas only available to subscribers. You can get access to all this exciting stuff by signing up for the newsletter here https://mailchi.mp/bf0d6fb45630/hnlloydnewsletter. And don't forget to like the Murder Tales Facebook page https://www.facebook.com/crimediscussion/.

Murder Tales:

My Bloody Valentine

By

H. N. LLOYD

Content

Introduction

What is love? Well, I can tell you that chemically love is our brain being flooded by a neurotrophin known as Nerve Growth Factor, or NGF. This protein is essential to the survival of sympathetic and sensory neurones. Without NGF, these brain cells would die. The key to understanding love is understanding that NGF is essential to ovulation. When we meet someone who is a good genetic match, our brain creates excessive amounts of NGF, which coats the sympathetic neurones in our brains, in women this then allows you to ovulate more readily and increases the chances of impregnation. The NGF protein creates all the stereotypical physical feelings of love, meaning that love is a chemical trick of the brain, an unfortunate side effect of our genetic imperative to pass on our genetic inheritance. It is in its most basic form a neurological chemical reaction which makes procreation easier. After a year of meeting our genetic match, the NGF levels in the brain begin to dissipate, after this point, we are strictly speaking no longer in love, anything that remains is, well, simply a bad habit that's difficult to kick, a bit like smoking.

This is, of course, a cynical scientific answer, which does not explain why love is so overpowering, such a force, such an all-consuming obsession. Love has caused wars, love has saved lives, love has spurred people to the heights of great heroism, and equally, it has dashed them to the depths of detestable destruction.

In this volume of Murder Tales, it is to those latter acts that we turn our attention. We shall look in horror at how love has destroyed all that is good and wholesome in people, how it has ruined and wrecked lives, how it has twisted people's minds so that they can carry out the most despicable and terrifying acts imaginable. Over the following blood-soaked pages, you will see the true cruelty, despair and depravity to which love can make people sink.

Enjoy.

The Quaker the Locomotive and the Apple Pip Defence: John Tawell and Sarah Hart

The murder of Sarah Hart by her lover John Tawell is so chock full of criminological firsts it's shocking that the case isn't better known. It was the first case where a killer used prussic acid to fell his victim. It was the first case where a killer used the power and speed of the locomotive engine to make good his escape and try to establish an alibi. Most notably of all, it's the first-ever case where a telecommunications device was used to directly identify and capture a killer.

John Tawell had always been a bit of a rum character, a man who put up a good public front but couldn't help letting his mask of respectability slip whenever the chance arose. From a good family who hailed from Beccles in Norfolk, Tawell spent his formative years learning to be a salesman. Learning an easy smile, an amicable personality, a friendly and approachable manner. By the age of fourteen, he had moved from the provinces to London to further his trade. He was encouraged by his employer to attend a "Friends" meeting at the local Quaker Meeting House, and Tawell could instantly see the chances for social networking and improving his business standing such an organisation could give him. The Quakers or the Religious Society of Friends to give them their proper name, formed in the 17th century when George Fox became unhappy with the manner in which the Church of England ministered to its flock. Fox felt that Jesus had become too marginalised in the teachings of the church. In Fox's mind, the Church of England had perverted hymns, sermons and even group prayers so that Jesus and his message were no longer the central idols at the heart of the religion. Fox also felt it was wrong to only have one ordained person in every town or village who was the local authority on religion and spirituality, for Fox believed Jesus was inside all of us. Therefore at Quaker meetings after a period of quiet stillness and reflection, anyone could stand and say a few words, or say a prayer, or read something they felt represented the true spirit and word of Jesus. Even women were encouraged to stand up and speak if the Lord moved them to. Not only did The Society of Friends encourage women to speak their mind, but they also opposed war, they opposed slavery, they opposed capital punishment, they opposed alcohol. Importantly they also believed in being humble, in wearing plain dark clothing, nothing fancy or expensive, nothing that showed one person was richer or of socially better standing than another. After all, Fox believed we were all equal in the eyes of Jesus. Of course, the established church didn't like this forward-thinking challenge to their spiritual supremacy. In 1650 George Fox was brought before his local magistrate for blasphemy, Fox bade the magistrates to "tremble at the word of the Lord." In response to this religious quote, the magistrate, Gervase Bennett, referred to Fox as a Quaker and the name stuck.

By 1800 the Quakers were a respectable and accepted offshoot of the Church of England, indeed many had realised how advantageous it could be to business to become one of the Friends, it was preferable for a Quaker to take his business to another Quaker if possible. This ensured that many Quakers prospered financially, and subsequently, many early banks were owned by Quakers. John Tawell attended his first meeting out of a desire to please his employer, he then saw the opportunities the Society of Friends gave him to increase his coffers, and soon after he became a regular attendee. Not that he stuck rigorously to the Friends doctrines. The Quakers had become somewhat inward-looking after the death of George Fox and the initial rapid expansion of the religion. After George Fox's death, some fairly peculiar doctrines began to set into the Society of Friends, such as one rule that said Quakers could only marry others

Quakers. Therefore the Friends were deeply displeased when in 1806 they learnt that John Tawell had seduced a servant girl called Mary Freeman and gotten her pregnant. This sin was made all the worse for the pregnant girl wasn't a Quaker. Tawell tried to do the honourable thing, and he married Mary. This marriage raised the ire of his Quaker brethren even further, and Tawell found himself being expelled from the Society of Friends.

Despite having being expelled from the Society of Friends Tawell still thought of himself as a Quaker, and he still dressed in their distinctive sombre garb, the characteristic dark greatcoat and wide-brimmed black hat. In other respects, he moved on with his life, and he got himself a position which would set him in good stead for the future, he became an assistant to a chemist. Here Tawell learnt all about the primitive medicinal curatives a 19th-century apothecary had to offer. It was mainly all old wives tales and placebos and dangerous quackery, but he learnt what ointments, emetics, laxatives and purgatives were usually used for what ailments and in what doses. Things were going very well for Tawell, he had a blossoming family, and he was earning an above-average wage, but Tawell was never very good with money. He seemed to always manage to fritter money away, and he always needed more of it. It was in 1814 due to this poor financial acumen Tawell got himself into hot water and showed his first penchant for criminal behaviour. Back in the early 19th century, most people had no need for paper money. Indeed, it was extremely rare outside of business that anyone would need or carry pecuniary notes of any kind. With an average weekly wage of about 10s, ordinary people going about their day to day lives could never dream of spending £1 in an entire week, let alone £10 or £20. Because of this paper money was a rare and glorified IOU issued by banks stating that the bank would honour the debt on behalf of the bearer at some later date. The note would be handed in at one business, and that business would then go back to the bank who had issued the note and claim that sum of money from the bank in gold. Tawell came a cropper when he was caught trying to pass off a forged £10 note allegedly issued by Smith's Bank of Uxbridge. The banknote, which would be worth about £500 by today's standards, was obviously forged, and Tawell found himself being immediately arrested. This was a serious matter in 1814, forgery was one of the many crimes on the statute books that was punishable by death. John Tawell was put on trial for his life and was promptly found guilty. Now, whether via luck or Tawell being clever when considering his victim, he avoided the death penalty. Smith's Bank was a Quaker-owned business, and they were dead against the death penalty. They protested that as the victim of the crime, they did not want the man who had sinned against them to lose his life. So, the Court showed Tawell leniency and instead, they decided to transport him to Australia for fourteen years.

Transportation was a feared sentence, it was viewed almost as fearfully as being executed. Even if someone was not transported for life, they had little hope of returning home. They had to survive a voyage on dangerous seas halfway around the world, they had to survive exotic diseases, they had to survive the flora and fauna of a little known and little-explored continent. If by some miracle they survived the oppressive heat, awful conditions, exotic diseases and illnesses, avoided the deadly bite of a snake, spider, shark or even something as innocuous as a mosquito, then at the end of their sentence there was one last horror. The now reformed criminal had to somehow find the money themselves to pay for a passage back to a country where their family had probably long forgotten them and moved on. Not surprisingly very few ever returned from a sentence of penal transportation. When a prisoner arrived at a penal colony, he or she were immediately given to one of the local landowners, and would thereupon be used effectively as a slave until their sentence expired, or they were given a "ticket of leave," which was a glorified governor's pardon. Treatment of prisoners was harsh and cruel, with little oversight from the Crown brutality and beatings were rife. Punishment for infringements of the strict but sometimes arbitrary rules set by the overseers was so severe they were likely to result in death.

With his "expertise" in medicine, Tawell was put to work as a medic in the convict's hospital. Here he kept his head down and worked hard, so much so that in 1820 he was granted his "ticket of leave." Tawell elected to stay in Australia as a free man, for he had seen a gap in the market. The penal colony didn't have a chemist, so, Tawell set himself up as one, and the money came rolling in, and pretty soon he owned a chain of chemists which encompassed every single penal colony in Australia. Tawell made enough money to contact his wife back in England, and send for her and their two children. They joined him in Australia, and Tawell set about making himself an indispensable pillar of the community. He was central to the formation of the first Quaker church in Australia and became one of the groups "elders" or religious leaders. He gave the Quakers their first Friends meeting house and began to hold sermons on the Sydney beach, mostly extolling the virtues of abstinence, during which pompous moralising addresses he would pour barrels of liquor into the sea.

Despite being extremely prosperous, and getting to enjoy some of the most glorious weather in the world, Mary Tawell pined for England, and so in 1831 the family moved back to their mother country, it was a move that John Tawell would later rue. It seems that the return to England was cursed. The children, no longer use to the inclement British weather and the industrial smog of London fell ill. Tawell's youngest son, William, died within two years of the return, their eldest son, John, died in 1838. Mary Tawell herself suffered as a result of the return, she contracted the dreaded and deadly consumption (tuberculosis). She fell desperately ill, and Tawell hired a nurse to care for his ailing wife, a woman called Sarah Lawrence. Tawell fancied the pants off Sarah Lawrence on sight, she was young and pretty, and despite her being over half his age he immediately set about seducing her. As his wife was lying on her death bed, Tawell was already secretly starting a new family with Sarah Lawrence.

Just a few short months after the death of their eldest son, Mary Tawell died. John Tawell sort solace in the arms of his lover and in the Society of Friends, but the London Quakers were wary of the ex-convict, and wouldn't let him fully back into their group. So, Tawell decided that if he could make a good enough impression with one or two very influential Quakers, then this would eventually open the door to his entering the wider society again. To this end, Tawell inveigled his way into the affections of a widowed Quaker called Sarah Cutforth. She was a respectable headmistress from Clerkenwell with good links to many of the elders in the London Quaker community. These elders disproved of the match, and despite the warnings of her fellow Quakers not to trust the felonious fellow, Sarah Cutforth married John Tawell in 1841. The marriage didn't stop Tawell from continuing his relationship with Sarah Lawrence. Tawell had installed his mistress in a cottage in the village of Salt Hill on the outskirts of Slough. He'd moved her away from London and possible discovery by using a rather cruel method. He'd told Sarah that he loved her deeply, but he could not marry her as she was not a Quaker, and therefore their love could jeopardise his fully re-entering the Circle of Friends and as a result his future business prospects. Sarah said she fully understood, and to try and make Tawell's life and ambitions easier Sarah agreed to "become dead to the world." She severed contact with all her old associates, she cut off contact with her family, including her dear old mum, and changed her name to Sarah Hart so that no one could trace her. Tawell hoped that with Sarah suitably isolated no one would ever discover he was having an illicit affair with a young girl half his age, and this damaging information would never find its way back to the Society of Friends. Having completely cut Sarah off from all whom she loved and held dear Tawell used Sarah for one purpose alone. Tawell would travel to Slough a few times every week where he would have sexual relations with Sarah. She mistook this relationship of convenience for love and bore Tawell two children. To sweeten the deal Tawell gave Sarah maintenance of £1 a week for the children's upkeep, this would equate to a measly £50 by today's standards.

By 1844 Tawell was struggling financially. His monopoly on Australia's medicinal market had been broken. Others had opened up chemist shops and had started undercutting Tawell's exorbitant prices. As a result, his affluent lifestyle was beginning to hit the rocks, and his good standing in the community was teetering on a knife's edge. With his finances so precarious he stopped paying Sarah Lawrence (or Hart as she now called herself) her £1 a week. So, in desperate need of the money, she went to her local Court and took out a Maintenance Order against Tawell, naming Tawell in the Court documents as the father of her two children. This was problematic for Tawell, it meant that the veneer of respectability he had built around himself could be ruined if anyone read the Court documents and found out about his mistress and illegitimate children. His hopes of ever being fully accepted back into the Society of Friends and the lucrative business this would bring his way would be gone forever. Of course, Tawell could see one easy way in which he could alleviate both his financial burdens and legal worries. If only Sarah Lawrence ceased to be his lover in a rather terminal fashion, then both the financial responsibility he owed to her and the problematic Court Order would disappear.

John Tawell New Year's resolution for 1845 was to uncomplicate his love life and thereby his finances. To no longer have an inconvenient and secret lover hanging like a loadstone around his neck. He brooded upon the matter and came up with a scheme which he thought was infallible. Tawell plotted to murder his lover, and then use the speed of the locomotive engine to get him back to London in time to create a reasonable alibi. On Wednesday the 1st of January 1845 John Tawell went to Hughes' Chemists on Bishopgate's Street and purchased two bottles of Steele's Acid, a varicose vein treatment which contained the active ingredient of prussic acid. After making his purchase, Tawell went to the Jerusalem Coffee Shop in Cowper's Court, in the city. Although it was a coffee shop, it was full of well to do bankers and businessmen, and Tawell was well known there. In fact, it is said that Tawell conducted most of his business from that particular coffee shop. At 4.00 pm. he left the establishment, leaving his jacket behind. This was an attempt to establish an alibi. For when he would return to collect it five hours later, he hoped that people would think it impossible that he would have been able to make the forty-mile round journey to Slough and back in such a few short hours. After all, these were the days when steam locomotives were still a relative novelty. Tawell rushed to Paddington Station where he boarded his train for Slough. He met Sarah at her idyllic little cottage bringing her a bottle of stout as a present, and he sat with her and watched with malicious glee as she glugged it down, for Tawell had laced the drink with the poisonous prussic acid.

Sarah's neighbour, a woman by the name of Mary Ann Ashley, heard a stifled scream coming from Sarah Hart's cottage, a heavy thump as if someone had fallen to the ground, and the sound of someone desperately gasping for air. She then saw John Tawell rush from the cottage. Thinking that the noises and the speed of Tawell's retreat were suspicious, Mrs Ashley decided to call upon Sarah to make sure that everything was alright. Mrs Ashley found Sarah lying on the floor of her cottage, grasping at her stomach, frothing at the mouth, writhing around in agony. She ran to get the village doctor, but by the time they both returned to the cottage, Sarah was dead. Mrs Ashley's screams and shouts as she ran through the village also brought the attention of a vicar, the Reverend E. T. Champnes from Upton-Cum-Chumley. He took Mrs Ashley's description of the killer, a man dressed as a Quaker in a dark overcoat and wide-brimmed hat, and he raced to the local train station arriving just in time to see Tawell jump onto the departing train for London. The Reverend Champnes accosted the Station Master, a man called Mr Howell and told him that a man on the train that had just departed had just murdered a woman in the village of Salt Hill. Mr Howell thought for a moment and realised just what he needed to do. The station had been equipped with one of the new telegraph machines, and this would allow him to send a message on ahead to

Paddington Station.   The Reverend and the Station Master went to the Station Masters Cottage, where the Station Master took his seat before the telegraph machine and sent the historic missive.

"A murder has just been committed at Salt Hill, and the suspected murderer was seen to take a first-class ticket to London by the train that left Slough at 7.42pm. He is in the garb of a Kwaker with a brown great coat on which reaches his feet. He is in the last compartment of the second first-class carriage."

Now, when this message was received at Paddington Station, the Station Master in the great metropolis struggled to understand what the provincial Station Master at Salt Hill was on about. He had no idea what a Kwaker was? So, he asked for the message to be sent again, again the word Kwaker appeared in the message, so he requested the message be sent a third time. It was only thanks to the intelligence of one of the station clerks that the message was eventually understood. This bright young man suggested that the Salt Hill Station Master might have typed the word Kwaker as the telegraph's machine's one failing was that it was incapable of sending a letter Q, they were, therefore, looking for a Quaker. With this revelation, the clerk was dispatched to the offices of the Great Western Railway Police, and Sergeant William Williams quickly put himself into plainclothes and began to mingle with the waiting passengers on the platform. Sure enough, when the train from Salt Hill pulled into the station, a man in the sombre garb of a Quaker stepped from the last compartment of the second first-class carriage. Sergeant Williams and the station clerk watched Tawell as he made his way to the New Road where he got onto an omnibus, and Sergeant Williams followed him. The station clerk raced back to his office, and with great excitement and satisfaction, he sent a message back to Salt Hill station:

"The up train has arrived, and a person answering in every respect the description given by the Telegraph

came out of the compartment mentioned. The man got into a New Road omnibus and Sergeant Williams into the same."

Sergeant Williams believed he was inconspicuous. However, he obviously had the air of officialdom about him and drew undue attention to himself, and Tawell mistook Sergeant Williams for a conductor and tried to pay him the 6d fare. Tawell got off the bus at Princes Street in the centre of the square mile of the city of London. Sergeant Williams trailed Tawell at a safer distance. Tawell went the short distance to Cornhill where he turned into Cowper's Court and popped into the Jerusalem Coffee Shop. Here Tawell had a warming cup of coffee, collected his purposefully misplaced jacket, and hoped that he had firmly established his alibi. As Tawell did this, Sergeant Williams waited dutifully outside until Tawell stepped back out into the bitterly cold night air. The dogged copper then followed Tawell from Cowper's Court to Birchin Lane and from there to

Scott's Yard where Tawell disappeared into the Friends Lodging House, a boarding house exclusively for Quakers. Sergeant Williams waited in the cold and dark for over an hour until he was confident that Tawell was not leaving the premises again that evening, only then did he make his way to Paddington Green Police Station. Here Sergeant Williams passed on all he had found to Chief Inspector Wiggins. Inspector Wiggins contacted Salt Hill and confirmed the circumstances of the case, after all, he didn't want to end up with egg on his face if it all turned out to be an embarrassing miscommunication.

The next morning, with all the circumstances correctly verified with the police at Salt Hill, Chief Inspector Wiggins summoned Sergeant Williams and asked him to accompany him back to Scott's Yard so that he could identify the suspect. The two coppers searched the area and eventually found Tawell back in the Jerusalem Coffee Shop. They approached the ageing Quaker and asked him what he knew of the murder in Slough the previous day, *"You must be mistaken, my station in life places me above suspicion,"* Tawell rather haughtily and defensively replied. Feeling the response was a little too dismissive and defensive the two police officers persisted. Tawell continued to deny all knowledge of the crime and stated adamantly that he hadn't left London the previous day. He even cheekily stated that the manager of the coffee shop they were stood in, along with several of the customers, would be able to give him a cast-iron alibi. Chief Inspector Wiggins was unmoved by the denials, and he arrested John Tawell on the spot.

Tawell hired Sir Fitzroy Kelly KC, the most lauded barrister of the day, a man who had just been appointed as Solicitor General. The problem was Sir Fitzroy was more used to commercial law, he was completely out of his depth when it came to criminal proceedings. He was confident in the defence that Tawell could not have made the forty-mile round journey to Slough and back, stopping off to poison Sarah Hart along the way, in the five-hour window available to Tawell. Unfortunately for Tawell and Sir Fitzroy; Chief Inspector Wiggins was diligent in his job. He successfully completed himself the so-called impossible journey he was accusing Tawell of making. He went from the Jerusalem Coffee Shop, catching the train at Paddington to Slough just after 4.00 p.m. He got off the train at Salt Hill, went to Sarah Hart's cottage where he spent a leisurely fifteen minutes relaxing, before making his way back to the Salt Hill Train Station, catching the return train to London and walking back to the Jerusalem Coffee Shop comfortably in time for the 9.00 p.m. deadline. With the alibi in tatters, Sir Fitzroy was forced to fall back on a second ridiculous defence that Tawell himself suggested. Tawell now admitted that he did know Sarah Hart, and that he had been her lover, but that he hadn't killed her, it was her love of apples that did for her. Tawell suggested that Sarah had ingested too many apple pips, causing her to succumb to prussic acid poisoning. When Mr Justice Baron Park opened the trial on Wednesday the 12th of March 1845 at Aylesbury County Court, Sir Fitzroy began the defence with those two words, apple pips. This defence was ludicrous and was laughed at, especially when it was shown the sheer number of apple pips Sarah Hart would have had to have ingested to have died in such a horrific manner. After a two-day trial, which mainly focused on the lethal qualities of apple pips, the jury retired and took just half an hour to convict John Tawell of murder, and Mr Justice Park had no option but to sentence Tawell to death. Sir Fitzroy Kelly was left with a lasting reminder of the murderer John Tawell, and he rued the day he ever took him on as a client. You see, from the day Sir Fitzroy ran with the ludicrous apple pip defence it blighted his career. Until the day he died, and no matter to what dizzying heights he reached in the legal profession, he was forevermore derisively known as "Apple-Pip" Kelly KC.

On the morning of Friday the 28th of March 1845, John Tawell made a full and frank confession to the murder of Sarah Hart. In fact, he even confessed to having tried to poison her in the September of 1844, but he hadn't used a sufficient dose of prussic acid, and he'd only caused her some immense stomach cramps and a bout of vomiting. Tawell was then led in a sombre procession back to Aylesbury Court House, where a gallows had been erected. A crowd of over ten thousand people had gathered to see the "apple pip murderer" be hanged. It was a botched job, the drop used by the hangman was not sufficient, and rather than his neck-breaking, it took Tawell nearly a quarter of an hour to be slowly strangulated by the hangman's noose.

A Brush With Death: Henry Wainwright and Harriet Lane

Henry Wainwright was the perfect example of Victorian moralistic double standards. He appeared to all the world to be an upstanding citizen, a respectable owner of a flourishing brush making business, a loving husband, and father to five adoring children. His business dealings were prospering so well his family lived in the luxurious surroundings of Tredegar Square in the London Borough of Tower Hamlets. He was tea-total and gave regular and rousing lectures at the local temperance society extolling the dangers of drink. He would warn all who would listen about the terrible vices such insalubrious activities can lead to. He was a religious man, a member of several religious organisations who attempted to bring solace and moral sustenance to the poor and downtrodden of London's east end via pious sermonising and acts of meagre charity. But Henry Wainwright had a terrible secret. He was a womaniser who couldn't keep his eyes from wandering away from the loving gaze of his wife. He was a terrible flirt whose roving eye fell daily upon the many pretty women he encountered and he couldn't help but try to slither his way into their affections and bedsheets. His usual dalliances were with the dancers from the Pavilion Theatre which was located next to his shop at 85 Whitechapel Road and opposite his warehouse at number 215. The woman who was to become his regular mistress he met not at the theatre but at a dressmakers shop, in Waltham Cross. Harriet Lane was just twenty-one years old and a dressmaker's assistant, Wainwright, was thirty-three, handsome and prosperous. He easily swept the impressionable and inhibited woman off her feet and seduced her.

All too quickly, Harriet fell pregnant with Wainwright's baby. She knew that Wainwright was already married and that he had five children with his wife, yet she didn't seem to mind, for Harriet had fallen head over heels in love with Wainwright. Harriet was besotted. I believe that at the start of their dalliances Wainwright genuinely loved Harriet, for he installed her in a house in Sidney Square, roughly a mile and a half from where his wife and children lived. Here Harriet was happy, her neighbours knew her as Mrs King, and believed that her husband, Percy, was a travelling salesman. Wainwright even furnished Harriet with a large thick gold wedding ring which she placed proudly on her finger in order to give some verisimilitude to their tale. Whenever "Percy" visited Harriet, everyone agreed that he cherished and doted on her. No one ever doubted that there was true and genuine love between the pair.

Harriet's neighbours grew to know Harriet as a woman who loved the finer things in life. Harriet had expensive tastes, she loved fine clothes, fine furnishings and fine dining. Indeed, Harriet's personal expenses were usually well in excess of £4 a week, that's over £200 by today's standards, this was before Wainwright even took into consideration the cost of the rent on the large townhouse.

Harriet was happy and in love. The times she spent with Wainwright was the happiest in her life. She doted on her bearded paramour. She didn't care if the marriage was an illusion. Her father wrote to Harriet on several occasions begging her to return to the family home and respectability, to leave the duplicitous adulterer to his own sordid and devious devices. Harriet demurred, and wrote back saying that Wainwright, *"treats me like a lady."* Over the next two years, the secret love affair continued with a growing passion and fervour. Harriet bore Henry a second illegitimate child, and the besotted young woman began to believe that she and her children were Wainwright's favoured family and number one priority. Oh, how wrong Harriett was.

By 1874 the love Wainwright held for Harriet had soured. Harriet had taken to drink, and she badgered Wainwright constantly for more money to fund her increasingly lavish and booze-soaked lifestyle. Maintaining two households in two affluent areas of the city was becoming too much of a burden for Wainwright. Harriet was wanting more and more money and had even begun to use Wainwrights double life as leverage to secure increased financial security from her lover. After all, how would Elizabeth Wainwright react if she found out her husband had fathered two more children to a kept woman not two miles from her own family home. Wainwright began to look for a way out of his extramarital relationship and came up with a rather cruel and unusual plan to rid himself of the lovelorn Harriet Lane.

Naturally, Harriet hadn't met any of Wainwrights family, what with her being his dirty little secret. So, when Henry Wainwright introduced Harriet to his brother,

Thomas, under the extraordinary nom de plume Teddy Frieake, she had no idea that Henry Wainwright had ordered his younger brother to seduce Harriet. Thomas Wainwright took to his task with alacrity, and pretty soon Harriet and Thomas were exchanging endearing little notes and having illicit encounters. Things seemed to move quickly, for, within a few weeks, Harriet was introducing Mr Frieake to her close friend and children's nanny, Mrs Wilmore. The Wainwright's plan was simple and malevolent. Thomas Wainwright was to persuade Harriet Lane to go on a lover's tryst with him to the continent, here Thomas Wainwright would abandon Harriet somewhere in the Mediterranean with no finances and no hope of ever returning to England. It was a cruel plan, but it didn't work for one simple reason, Harriet still loved the bones of Henry Wainwright, and couldn't bring herself to abandon her married lover for another suitor.

With the original plan failing abysmally, Henry Wainwright decided upon more desperate measures. At 4.00 p.m. on Friday the 11th of September 1874 Harriet Lane attended the warehouse at 215 Whitechapel Road, where she had arranged to meet Teddy Frieke (AKA Thomas Wainwright) for one final secret lover's rendezvous. A little time later some workmen working out on the Whitechapel Road heard gunshots coming from somewhere in the vicinity of the warehouse located at number 215. Later that day Henry Wainwright attended the home address of Mrs Wilmore. Wainwright appeared to be distressed and informed Mrs Wilmore that Harriet had left him, she had eloped with Teddy Frieke and intended to make a new life for herself with him in Brighton. This new life did not include the children she had borne with Henry Wainwright. Wainwright promptly came to terms with Mrs Wilmore for her continued care of his children, at a price which greatly reduced the overheads he had incurred when his mistress had been the children's primary career. For eight months

Mrs Wilmore received £5 a month from Mr Wainwright (about £250 by today's standards), then in July of 1875 the payments stopped, and Mrs Wilmore heard not one more word from Mr Wainwright. Soon after, however, Mrs Wilmore received a telegram purporting to be from Teddy Frieke thanking her for her continued care of Harriet's children and stating that he and Harriet were moving to Paris.

Despite his reduced expenses now he was free of his mistress and illegitimate children, Henry Wainwright still found his business interests financially struggling. Not even a substantial contract to provide the whole of the Metropolitan Police Force with chloride of lime could save Wainwright's finances. So, he took steps to save the business. In February 1875 he reduced the number of staff he employed to the bare minimum he needed to keep the business going. When this didn't work, Wainwright turned to fraud, attempting to burn down his shop and collect on the insurance money. The ploy failed, foul play was instantly suspected, and the insurance company refused to pay out on the policy. By Saturday the 11th of September 1875 it had become necessary for Wainwright to sell the warehouse at number 215 Whitechapel Road and move his workshop and goods to smaller and less convenient premises across the river Thames in Southwark, a building called the Hen and Chickens which was leased to his brother, Thomas. On the day of the move across the river, Wainwright reemployed the services of one of his former employees, a young man called Alfred Phillip Stokes. Stokes first job of the day was to get rid of a dirty axe, a hammer and a shovel. Wainwright wanted Stokes to sell these instruments to a man called Mr Martins, who was taking over the warehouse from Wainwright. Stokes asked why Mr Wainwright didn't just leave the tools behind for Mr Martin to find for himself, but Wainwright was insistent that Stokes should pretend the tools were his own and barter a good price for them. Wainwright seemed quite keen to distance himself as much as he could from the filthy implements. Once Stokes had disposed of the dubious tools, Wainwright asked the young man to carry from the warehouse two heavy parcels wrapped in American canvas, and wait for him in Vine Yard, (the courtyard at the back of the warehouse) while Wainwright summoned a carriage. Stokes was taken by the overpowering smell of putrefaction that oozed nauseously from the packages. Indeed, it was a smell that many in the neighbourhood had been complaining about for several months, and all had assumed was coming from the Wainwright's warehouse. Curiosity suddenly got the better of Stokes, he unwrapped one the packages and peered inside. It was with a racing heart, and a repressed scream that Stokes hastily resealed the pack, for inside was the severed arm and head of a young woman.

Stokes was scared for his life. He realised he was alone in a dark warehouse with a murderer. In order to ensure his safety, Stokes resolved to help his former employer into a carriage with the foul-smelling package, and then find the nearest policeman and report what he'd discovered. Presently, Wainwright returned with a cab and asked Stokes to lift the packages into the carriage. He then expected Stokes to get into the carriage with him so that when they arrived at the Hen and Chickens, his ex-employee could help him unload the heavy packages and carry them into the new premises. Stokes suddenly found his mouth dry and his hands shaking, as with fear and trepidation he went to climb into the carriage, then fortune smiled upon him. Wainwright spotted a chorus and dancing girl from the Pavilion Theatre who he'd been eyeing as a potential new mistress for quite some time. Wainwright called out to Alice Dash and offered her a joy ride in his carriage. She agreed, and Wainwright helped her up into the vehicle so that she could sit beside him. Lighting a cigar to mask the frightful smell of death Wainwright ordered Stokes to meet him at 7.00 p.m. that evening at the Hen and Chickens where they would conclude their business. With these parting instructions, the hansom carriage pulled away along the Whitechapel High Street towards the Commercial Road. Stokes did not rest on his laurels or thank his lucky stars for his miraculous escape, he immediately jumped into action. He hared off down the road after the carriage, running pell-mell to keep up with the horse-drawn vehicle. Stokes was a massive sweating and breathless mess as he ran all the way along the Aldgate High Street into Leadenhall Street where finally he saw a Police Constable on his beat. Stokes ran to the officer and breathlessly told him his story. The officer chastised Stokes for being drunk and mad and telling tales and told him in no uncertain terms to be on his way. Dismayed and in great discomfort from his great run, Stokes was forced to continue his desperate race after the carriage. He crossed London Bridge and began to run down the Borough High Street, where the cab pulled to a stop near the London and Country Bank. Here, Stokes mercifully saw another police officer. He ran directly to Police

Constable Henry Turner and told him his tale. PC Turner took Stokes' story with all seriousness, and he approached the cab. PC Turner asked Wainwright what was inside the parcel he was carrying, to which Wainwright replied with a conspiratorial wink, *"Say nothing, ask no questions and there's £50 in it for you."* PC Turner was now more intrigued than ever after the offered bribe and reached into the carriage to examine one of the parcels, at which point Wainwright appeared to become quite panicked, and he began to squawk in quite an alarmed tone, *"Don't, for goodness sake, don't touch it! Let me go; I will give you £200."* Ignoring this second offer of a bribe PC Turner determinedly unwrapped one of the parcels and like Stokes before him saw the head of a young woman staring up at him. Both Wainwright and Alice Dash were immediately arrested for murder[i].

The dismembered and decomposing body was taken to St Saviours Dead-house where Police Surgeon Fredrick George Larkin carried out a post-mortem. He discerned that the body had been crudely cut apart by someone with no knowledge of anatomy. An attempt had been made to use lime to speed up the decomposition of the body, however, like many a killer in the annals of crime Wainwright had used slake lime which had in fact slowed down the process of putrefaction, preserving it rather starkly and making identification remarkably easy. Dr Larkin concluded that the victim had been shot three times in the back of the head with a small calibre weapon, the killer had also slashed the victim's throat with such ferocity that the windpipe had been severed in two.

Wainwright and Alice Dash had been taken to Stones End Police Station where they were interviewed by Chief Inspector Fox. Wainwright told Inspector Fox a likely story, he was completely innocent of any wrongdoing.

He had not known that the packages had contained the dismembered body of a young lady, he had been paid £5 by a man whose name he did not know who he had met in a pub to take the parcels to the Hen and Chickens. Meanwhile, uniformed police officers attended Wainwright's warehouse at 215 Whitechapel Road. Here they found the evidence they needed to prove Wainwright was lying. Several of the floorboards on the ground floor of the warehouse were found to be loose, and when removed a shallow grave was discovered, bits of flesh and slake lime still lingered in the hole. Mixed with the dirt and lime were a large gold wedding ring and a pair of earrings. Stokes then told the police of the tools Wainwright had asked him to sell. These tools were recovered from the man Stokes had sold them too, and were discovered to have blood and tiny pieces of flesh mixed in with the general dirt and filth that covered them. Evidently earlier that day, they had been used to dismember the corpse.

The police had to establish the identity of the dead woman. This turned out to be an easier job than they first assumed it might be. Harriet Lane's father read of the circumstances of Wainwright's arrest in the paper and immediately knew that the dead woman was his missing daughter. He went straight to the police to tell them that his daughter had been seduced and corrupted by Wainwright some three years before, and had disappeared about twelve months ago, allegedly running off to the continent with Teddy Frieake. Mr Lane told the police that his daughter had lived under the name of King, and gave them the details of her old address. Further investigations in this neighbourhood quickly led to Mrs Wilmore, and Wainwright's two abandoned illegitimate children. Mrs Wilmore told the police of Harriet's expensive tastes and of Wainwright's financial fall from grace and his eventual filing for bankruptcy. Ah-ha money was always a good motive for murder. The body had been so well externally preserved by the slake lime that Mr Lane was able to positively identify the body as that of his daughter, and Mrs Wilmore was able to identify the gold wedding ring and earrings found in the grave as belonging to Harriet King AKA Harriet Lane. With this evidence, the police lost little time charging Henry Wainwright with Harriet Lane's murder[ii].

The police were thorough in their job. Seeing as Teddy Frieake had played such an active part in the last few weeks of Harriet's life they traced him, he was an auctioneer and had been friends with the Wainwright brothers. Mrs Wilmore was positive that this Teddy Frieake was not the man she had been introduced to by Harriet. Further, this Teddy Frieake informed the police that he had fallen out with the Wainwright brothers when he discovered that Wainwright's mistress had been courting a man named Teddy Frieake. He was convinced that the Wainwrights had misappropriated his name for some illegal and fraudulent purpose. The question remained who had been posing as Teddy Frieake the year before? Thomas Wainwright had known a lot about "the other" fraudulent Teddy Frieake. Thomas had tried to placate the auctioneer when he'd complained about the misappropriation and use of his name. It had been Thomas Wainwright who had assured Frieake that his namesake did actually live on the other side of the River Thames, and told Frieake that his namesake was a rakish billiards player and quite the cad. If Thomas Wainwright had known so much about Teddy Frieake, the police obviously needed to talk to Thomas to find out more. Thomas Wainwright was brought in for questioning, and this led to his being identified as the man who had been posing as Teddy Frieake. Handwriting analysis also proved Thomas Wainwright was the man who had written all of the Frieake letters to Harriet, including the one which had lured Harriet to her death. Thomas Wainwright was charged with Being an Accessory to Murder.

Henry and Thomas Wainwright's trial took place at the Old Bailey before Mr Justice Cockburn, the Lord Chief Justice. The case against the pair was watertight. Now that the identity of the body could be conclusively proved as that of Wainwright's lover, his defence of having being given the package by a man he didn't know in a pub appeared more ludicrous than ever. Yet, Wainwright stuck with this defence. He was the victim of a terrible and damning coincidence. The inevitable outcome of the trial was, of course, a Guilty verdict, which duly came on Thursday the 2nd of December 1875. Thomas Wainwright was handed down a seven-year sentence for being an Accessory to Murder. Of course, Henry Wainwright faced a much harsher justice. When asked if he had anything to say before his inevitable sentence was passed, Henry Wainwright found himself unable even at that late juncture to admit his guilt:

"I will simply say that, standing as I now do upon the brink of eternity, and in the presence of that God before

whom I shall shortly appear, I swear that I am not the murderer of the remains found in my possession. I swear that I have never in my life fired a pistol. I swear also that I have not buried these remains, and that I did not exhume or mutilate them as has been proved before you by witnesses. I have been guilty of great immorality. I have been guilty of many indiscretions, but as for the crime of which I have been brought in guilty, I leave this dock with a calm and quiet conscience. My Lord, I thank you for the patience with which you have listened to me."

After these blatant lies had been uttered by Wainwright, Mr Justice Cockburn responded with his customary bluff coldness:

"You have been found guilty, in my opinion, upon the clearest and most convincing evidence of the murder of Harriet Louisa Lane, which has been laid to you charge. No one, I think, who has heard this trial can entertain the slightest shadow of a doubt of your guilt; and I can only deplore that, standing as you surely are upon the brink of

eternity, you should have called God to witness the rash assertion which has just issued from your lips. There can be no doubt that you took the life of this poor woman, who had been on the closest and most intimate terms of familiarity and affection with you, and who was the mother of your two children... It was a barbarous, cruel, inhuman and cowardly act. I do not wish to say anything to aggravate the position in which you stand, nor to dwell upon the enormity of your guilt, further than that by so doing I may rouse you to a sense of the position in which you stand, in which all hope of earthly mercy is cut off... I have to warn you against any delusive hope of mercy... therefore, prepare for the doom which awaits you. I have now only to pass upon you the dread sentence of the law, which is that you be taken from hence to the place whence you came, thence to a legal place of execution to be there hanged by the neck till you shall be dead, and that your body be buried within the precincts of the gaol in which you shall be last confined after your conviction, and may the Lord have mercy upon your soul."

On Tuesday the 21st of December 1875 a small invited crowd had gathered outside of the famed and dreaded Newgate Gaol. Henry Wainwright was led into the prison courtyard as the bells of St Sepulchre Church rang eight. He was led up to the gallows, and as he looked out at the gathered crowd, he cursed bitterly, "*So you curs, you've come to see a man die have you.*" Wainwright was to be executed by the famed hangman William Marwood, who had developed the "long drop" method of execution. Here the subject of the gallows had a long sharp drop that instantly broke the neck, ensuring a quick and painless death. However, it seems that Wainwright hadn't quite perfected his system, for it was said that Wainwright "died hard" and thrashed around for several minutes at the end of the rope, much to the joy of the baying crowd.

Burning Love

As the saying goes, the past is a foreign land, where customs and beliefs are stranger than anything we may see today. This brief little tale highlights this truth starkly and should make us grateful for the more enlightened times we now find ourselves living in.

Hannah and Timothy Simm no doubt loved each other at some juncture, they had been married for seven years, and in that time the love they had once held for each other had withered and died and turned into a bickering resentment. The year was 1894, long before television and radio worked as a handy distraction from the slow stultifying death of any tenderness and romance in a relationship. A time when the death knell of marriage could be heard ringing loud and clear, as there were no amusements to detract from the loveless sham a life together becomes. On Saturday the 27th of April 1894 the neighbours of forty-seven-year-old Hannah and Fifty-year-old Timothy Simm could hear the couple arguing through the paper-thin walls of their terrace house. The argument grew to a crescendo of shouts and hurled abuse until suddenly and unexpectedly an ear-piercing scream came through the walls, making the neighbours jump out of their skins. Outside their home in Stable Row, Bolton, England, passersby watched agog as Hannah Simm ran out into the cold night air, her body ablaze, her entire form engulfed in an inferno. A quick-thinking neighbour ripped off his overcoat, ran towards the aflame Mrs Simm, he wrapped his overcoat around her extinguishing the fires that consumed her. Mrs Simm fell to the cobbled ground, still screaming, more from shock, seeing as her burns were so bad they had probably damaged the nerve endings. From their house, Mrs Simm's daughter, an issue from a previous marriage named Mary Whittle, ran to her mother's side. "Who did this?" Miss Whittle asked, before Mrs Simm's accusing eyes came to rest upon her husband. He now stood shiftily behind Miss

Whittle, as Mrs Simm spat with contempt, "Timmy." As Mrs Simm uttered these words, Timothy Simm took to his heels.

Mrs Simm was taken to hospital where doctors examined the burns that covered the whole extent of her body, and they quickly decided that there was nothing they could do. Mrs Simm's life was in the hands of fate. The police attended Mrs Simm's bedside and asked for an account of what had happened. Mrs Simm informed the police that she and her husband had been arguing, Timothy Simm was a violent man, who often threatened in his drunken rages to murder his wife. This night as she cooked his supper of eggs and bacon, Timothy Simm had picked up the frying pan and smashed it over Mrs Simm's head, knocking her into a nearby chair. Concussed for a moment, when she gathered her senses, Timothy Simm was looming over her, lighting his pipe. Instead of extinguishing the paper he had used to light it, he threw the burning embers into Mrs Simm's lap, igniting her highly flammable dress. As she went up in a WHOOF of flames, Timothy Simm had stood in the kitchen dementedly screaming 'BURN! BURN!', as his wife staggered aflame from the kitchen, and out into the street. Two days after the murderous attack, Mrs Simm died.

Timothy Simm had fled to Wigan, his description had been so widely circulated for such an unusually cruel and callous murder, he was easily identified, and arrested by a local copper. He denied the charges and stated that he'd accidentally dropped the paper into his wife's lap as he'd passed it to her so that she could light her own pipe. It didn't seem a very likely story, especially seeing as Simm had already lied to the police, giving them a false name and address upon arrest, and then had attempted to escape from the police van as he was brought in for questioning.

Simm's trial at Manchester Assizes, before Mr Justice Kennedy, was brief, perfunctory and very, very peculiar. After hearing Simms side of the events, Mr Justice Kennedy decided that there wasn't a case of murder to answer and instead decided that Simm should stand trial for manslaughter. Mr Justice Kennedy then continued his peculiar antics by questioning the police as to why they had not let Simm cross-examine his mortally wounded wife on her deathbed, and challenge her story for lies. It seems that Mr Justice Kennedy was of the belief that it was every abusive husband's right to harangue their dying wives in their final moments. The police were unable to give an answer that the peculiar judge liked, and as a result, the extremely contrary Mr Justice Kennedy instructed the jury there and then to go away and consider their verdict, preferably one favourable to Timothy Simm. The jury duly did so, and within a few short minutes, they returned with a Not Guilty verdict in Simm's favour.

So there we are. I have no doubt that Timothy Simm was guilty of the most horrendously cruel murder of his wife. Yet, in the days when a wife was seen as her husband's property, the judge and jury were inclined to believe the words of the master of the house, over those of the pained and dying woman.

The Inconvenient Husband

Love and desire go hand in hand, yet when love and an illicit desire merge it can be an explosive combination in which someone, usually an innocent party, dies, all because they are an inconvenient barrier to the fruition of love and the desire of its sexual fulfilment.

Edith Thompson nee Graydon was a young, headstrong, determined girl, talented and indomitable, yet she also filled her head with slushy romantic literature which through her impressionable years gave her unreasonable expectations of what to expect from normal adult relationships. She was born on Christmas day 1893, she was the daughter of a clerk for the Imperial Tobacco Company, and from a young age, she showed a natural aptitude for her father's talent with numbers. She was also artistic, with a gift for dancing, acting and languages. The world was her oyster, and she set out to prove herself. Upon leaving school at fourteen, she became a bookkeeper for a milliner, where her natural gifts for numbers and languages marked her out as something special. She was quickly promoted to Chief Buyer, where her fluent French made her invaluable in the company's regular business dealings with French suppliers, and soon she was earning more money than her father. In 1909 aged just fifteen she met eighteen-year-old Percy Thompson, and she fell head-over-heels in love with him. Both sets of parents disagreed with the match-up, Percy was seen as a chain-smoking bit of rough by the Graydon's, Edith was considered to be impetuous, overly salacious and improper by the Thompsons. The Thompsons became enraged when against all standards of decency Edith scandalously took Percy on holiday to Cornwall, un-chaperoned. The union was indeed a folly of youth, the pair should never have married. Percy Thompson wasn't the romantic hero of Edith's literature, he might have seemed like the coarse romantic Heathcliff to an impressionable young mind, but when locked into marriage, Percy simply came across as boring and boorish. The pair courted for six years, an unfeasibly long time in those bygone Edwardian days, and indeed no one doubts that they had consummated their relationship long before the end of this courtship. Edith and Percy married in 1916, Percy was imminently due to be conscripted and sent off to fight in the trenches of the First World War. Percy lucked out on this occasion, after joining the London Scottish Regiment, he was diagnosed by Army doctors as having a heart condition, something that wasn't helped by his slightly problematic waistline and his fifty a day smoking habit. He was discharged and allowed to return to his wife and Edith's family, who the newlyweds had been forced to live with. Percy didn't like living with Edith's family, of course, they had made it plain that they weren't happy with Percy finally making an "honest" woman out of their beloved daughter. So, shortly after his return, the newlyweds moved to the seaside retreat of Westcliff On Sea, a small town on the Thames Estuary, close enough to London for them both to commute to their daily jobs in the city. They stayed there until the end of the war when Edith grew tired of the boredom the small town held for one so vibrant and exuberant as her, and the couple moved back to London, 41 Kensington Garden's, Ilford.

The boredom and drudgery of married life continued to grate on Edith, and she began to look for some small escape elsewhere, so she turned to one of her loves from before married life, amateur dramatics. Am-dram isn't exactly a pastime that is conducive to a harmonious married life. The eager amateur actor often can find themselves mistaking the channelled emotions of a part for real feelings of love and desire, or even loathing. I have some knowledge of this, for a period I took up acting under the tutelage of a relatively well-known actress. Under her guidance, I turned to an amateur dramatics society to hone my somewhat none existent acting skills, and I discovered for myself what a hotbed of flirtation and sexual tension this arena can be. Of course, it suited Edith down to the ground, even if it did raise the eyebrows of one or two disproving neighbours.

Edith managed to resist the temptations of an am-dram romance, but the highly charged emotions of a holiday romance were a different story. Edith first met Frederick Bywaters in 1920, he was just eighteen years old at the time, a laundry steward on board the P & O ship S.S. Morea, he was a friend of Edith's brother, and was a potential suitor for Edith's sister Avis. Percy liked Freddy Bywaters, to begin with. He was an affable young cove, and the pair had something in common. Percy was, of course, a shipping clerk and his father had been a master mariner, and with Freddy working onboard ships, travelling the world, they enjoyed conversations about boats and sailing and all matters nautical. The friendship between the pair grew friendlier, and in 1921 Percy made a decision that ultimately was to prove fatal. Percy and Edith were taking Avis on holiday to the Isle of White, and Percy felt that this would be the perfect opportunity for Freddy to get to know Avis a bit better, perhaps woo Avis somewhat, and finally, perhaps, propose matrimony. With Percy and Edith chaperoning Avis, everyone agreed it was a fantastic idea, and Freddy readily agreed to join the trio. Unfortunately, he wasn't so much interested in Avis Graydon, as in something else that might have been on offer. It was as Edith and Avis watched a penny peepshow in a fairground that Freddy Bywaters made his move, as Avis was distracted by the distinctly naughty fun of the penny slot machine, Freddy took Edith aside and kissed her, and he was pleased when Edith responded rather favourably. As Edith and Freddy embarked on their affair, they must have laughed uproariously behind Percy's back when at the end of the holiday Percy suggested that Freddy took up lodgings with him and Edith back in Ilford. Freddy agreed with zeal, and so the scene was set for one of the most infamous murders of the 20th century.

The affair continued with gusto once Freddy was installed in Kensington Gardens. The couple would meet in parks and teashops, stealing kisses, and when in the parks sometimes more than just kisses, when they thought no one was looking. The only problem was people were looking, the adulterous couple were beginning to get noticed. The local gossip mongers began to talk about Edith Thompson and her relationship with the young lodger. The rumours began to filter back to Percy, who was beginning to grow increasingly miffed by the salacious tone of the stories. Things came to a head on Monday the 29th of August 1921, Percy had become increasingly sullen and withdrawn over the previous days. Edith had suggested that they all sit out in the garden and enjoy the warm summer weather. Percy lounged in a deckchair casting dark glances towards his wife and her lover. When Edith announced that she needed a hairpin, Freddy jumped to his feet from where he had laid on the grass and ran eagerly into the house to fetch one. Percy sneered at this and made a few disparaging comments to his wife who took umbrage with her husband's tone, by the time Freddy returned to the garden the Thompson's were having a full-blown argument over Edith's inappropriate relationship with Freddy. As Edith protested and told Percy not to be so silly, the argument grew in anger and vitriol. Eventually, Percy reached the end of his very short tether and hit Edith. Freddy unwilling to see his lover abused in such a way intervened and struck Percy, soon a fistfight raged in the garden between the pair, with Edith trying to separate the two circling dogs as they attempted to mark their territory. Of course, there really could only have been one winner, Percy Thompson. He got the better of the younger, impetuous, man, and threw Freddy out on his ear, with the definite impression being made that Percy never wanted to see sight nor sound of the young whippersnapper again. This might have been Percy's desire, but it certainly wasn't Edith's, and the affair continued.

Edith and Freddy would meet after Edith had finished work, meeting in the teashops of London, where they would steal a kiss or feel the frisson of charged love as their hands met over a warm teapot. Then the pair made a decision which would condemn them both, they began the overly heated correspondence that so incriminated them later in court. Over the next year, Edith sent Freddy sixty-two letters filled with excessively romantic tripe and indications of a growing and alarmingly faltering grip on reality. We don't know how many letters Freddy sent back in return, for Edith had the foresight to burn the replies. Young, naive, love-struck Freddy kept the letters Edith sent him, despite their incriminating content. From September to October 1921, Freddy was out at sea when he returned to England he had a new resolve. Freddy went straight round to Kensington Gardens and remonstrated with Percy demanding that he give Edith a divorce. "I don't see that it concerns you," Percy replied sneeringly. Freddy explained his deep love for Edith, and that it was painfully obvious to even the most casual of observers that the love between Edith and Percy was dead. Percy simply listened with mounting anger before replying, "Well, I've got her, and I shall keep her."

Edith was merely an object, a pawn in a cruel game Percy was playing to blight the hearts of Freddy Bywaters and Edith, sour grapes leading to sour games. Freddy left dejected and heartbroken, it seemed that his desired goal of being with Edith for the rest of their lives was further away than ever before. Percy would never consent to a divorce, and the fact began to play on young Freddy's mind.

When Freddy sailed away again, the correspondence between him and Edith began to take on a distinctly darker tone. Edith began to ask Freddy to procure her quinine, to place in Percy's food, she also started to send newspaper articles to Freddy about poisoning cases. At home Percy seemed to believe that Edith's infatuation with the young sailor was passing, Edith wrote to Freddy telling him:

"He said he was beginning to think both of us would be happier if we had a baby, I said no, a thousand times no. He began to question me and plead with me, Oh darling it's all so hard to bear. Come home to me, come quickly and help me. It's so much worst this time, you know I always sleep to the wall darlingest, well I still do, but he puts his arm around me, and oh, it's horrid."

As Edith portrayed the role of the loving wife to Percy, she secretly aborted a baby, which Freddy was in all probability the father of. Edith wrote to Freddy telling him the news. Her letters to Freddy continued in their dark meanderings, describing how Edith had started to put poison in Percy's insomnia medicine, and ground-up glass from a broken light bulb in his mashed potatoes. Yet, her greatest wish was for Freddy to return to her, like a knight in shining armour, these maudlin sentiments filled the pages:

'Darlingest I've surrendered to him unconditionally now, do you understand me? I think it the best way to disarm suspicion, in fact, he several times asked me if I am happy now, I said yes quite, but you know that's not the truth, don't you? If only I had you here to put my head on your shoulders and just sleep and dream and forget. Darlingest come to me soon, I want you so badly more and more'.

Soon after this missive, Edith reported to Freddy how she had aborted a second child. This time, the child was fathered by her long-suffering husband. Freddy returned to England in September of 1923, and duly brought with him the quinine that Edith had asked for, the couple began to meet in Wanstead Park, where they enjoyed copulation alfresco style. This romantic encounter Edith found particularly exhilarating, writing to Freddy in florid detail about how she had an orgasm as they frolicked naked on the heath:

"It seems a great welling up of love, of feeling, of inertia, just as if I am wax in your hands, to do with as you will, and I feel that if you do as you wish, I shall be happy."

Freddy went back to sea for a short period and returned on Tuesday the 3rd of October 1922. That very evening, after Edith had finished work, the couple met at Fuller's Tea Shop. Now, this meeting was important, it played a crucial role in the couple's downfall, the couple maintained that this was simply an innocent meeting where two lovers, who had not seen each other for several weeks, enjoyed each other's company. Those of a more suspicious bent believed that it was at this meeting that the couple plotted and conspired the final demise of Percy Thompson.

Shortly after midnight that evening Edith and Percy came out of Ilford train station, they had spent that evening with some friends at the theatre. As they walked along

Belgrave Road, a man rushed out of the shadows and attacked Percy, stabbing him three times in the neck with a clasp knife. The assailant was heard to shout, "Why don't you get a divorce, you cad!" Edith stood with her hands clasped to her mouth a look of horror on her face as she shouted at the assailant, "Oh, don't! Oh, don't!"

When help arrived, Edith told the paramedics that Percy had suffered a seizure, had fallen over and banged his head, it was an obvious lie. With noticeable stab wounds in the victim's neck, the police quickly became involved, and they were under no delusions that this was a murder inquiry. They spoke with Edith, who told them that she knew of no one who would want to harm her husband. Edith's neighbours told the police a different story. They had been scandalised by the young strumpet's behaviour over the past few years, and they were only too happy to tell the police about the old lodger who had been having an affair with Mrs Thompson, and about the time the lodger had punched Mr Thompson in the garden for all to see. The police went straight around to Freddy's parent's house, where Freddy was lodging. Here they discovered some bloodied clothes and the box of incriminating love letters. They arrested Freddy and took him to Ilford police station, where Edith saw Freddy for the first time since the murder, upon seeing him she broke down and announced tearfully, "Oh god, why did he do it? I never wanted him to do it!" This was a tremendous climb down for a woman who only a few months before had been asking her lover to procure poisons for her, and who had described in detail how she was poisoning her husband's food and medication. Freddy immediately admitted to the murder and was very forthcoming with his reasons as to why he had done away with Percy, "The reason I fought with Thompson was because he never acted like a man to his wife. He always seemed several degrees lower than a snake." Now if you ever find yourselves in the untenable position of being accused of murdering a love rival, take my advice and reframe from referring to the poor murder victim as a snake, or any other such comparable, it never sits well with judges or juries, and it'll probably go badly for you. Freddy, however, was unrepentant, "I loved her and could not go on seeing her live that life."

It seemed like a clear-cut case, Freddy Bywaters had been driven mad with lust and murdered the one person who was standing in the way of his having a long and happy life with the woman he loved. Edith Thompson might not have come out of the whole situation exactly smelling of roses, but she certainly hadn't committed the murder of Percy Thompson. Edwardian society was a very different place to our own, and a woman who could so heartlessly have an affair behind her husband's back, and abort unborn babies, well surely she was the type of person who could be capable of murder, and therefore surely such a person should be punished. So the police turned their attention to that fateful meeting at Fullers Tea Shop, the meeting between the murderer and the victim's wife that had taken place just a few hours before the murder. The police decided that it must have been at this location that Edith persuaded the otherwise mild-mannered Freddy Bywater to kill Percy Thompson, so the police charged Edith Thompson with murder as well. The police needed more evidence to prove Edith's murderous intent, and so Sir Bernard Spilsbury, that brilliant and famous pathologist, was called upon to carry out an autopsy on Percy Thompson, specifically to look for poisons or evidence of glass in his intestines. He found...absolutely nothing. Percy hadn't been poisoned, there was no glass in his intestines, the whole story was a wild fantasy made up by an impressionable young woman wanting to impress her equally impressionable lover.

The press roundly turned against Edith in those early days, for a time she became the most reviled woman in the country, an adulterating abortionist who led an innocent young man to murder due to her sexual powers over him. Edith was dubbed in the tabloids 'the Messalina of Ilford', and there was a belief held by just about everyone that she was about to get her just desserts. Indeed the judge who was selected to oversee the trial hoped to give Edith Thompson just that, moral and upstanding Mr Justice Montague Shearman was a bluff old fashioned man who believed in old-fashioned values, he was a sportsman and founder member of the Amateur Athletics Association. He believed in the sanctity of marriage, and that wives should be faithful and dutiful, and certainly shouldn't get daft romantic notions stuck in their noggin, they certainly shouldn't run around having affairs, that was the prerogative of men.

The trial began on Wednesday the 6th of December 1922, at the Old Bailey. During the trial, something remarkable began to happen, the tide of public opinion began to shift in Edith's favour. This in no small part was due to Freddy Bywaters. He remained steadfastly loyal to

Edith, testifying to what a brute Percy Thompson was, to how he stifled Edith and beat her. To how Percy and Edith were madly, deeply truly in love, most fervently of all he testified to how Edith had no knowledge of his actions. How he had acted alone and without persuasion from Edith. After all the good work Freddy had put into trying to get Edith's neck out of the hangman's noose, Edith went and firmly put it back in when she, against her counsel's wishes, took the stand. She came across badly, very badly. She came across as flighty and flirty, and she contradicted herself and was caught out telling damn right lies on several occasions. As she talked of her great love for Freddy, Mr Justice Shearman wrote in his ledger, "Great love, nonsense, great and wholesome disgust." The jury also took an instant dislike to the woman, and this was before the jury had turned their attention to those incriminating letters.

Ah yes, those letters, it was a bit of a stitch-up job all in all when it came to those letters being read out in court.

Most of the letters dealt with the drudgery of Edith's life, her daily toils at work, and the domestic situation of her home life. The jury wasn't told of this, it was made out to the jury that the letters were a constant hotbed of sin, deceit and murderous intent. Most of the letters were held back because it was felt some were too explicit, talking about Edith's menstruation cycle, and the power of Edith and Freddy's lovemaking, other letters simply held nothing to help the prosecution case. Later the foreman of the jury was to tell the press, "It was my duty to read them (the letters) to the members of the jury, 'nauseous' is hardly strong enough to describe their contents, Mrs Thompson's letters were her own condemnation." It seemed inevitable that the verdict would go against Edith, when the jury retired on Monday the 11th of December 1922, they deliberated for just two hours, before returning guilty verdicts for both Edith and Freddy. Edith let out a cry of horror and ran towards her father, arms outstretched, "Take me home, dad! Take me home!" She cried, Freddy jumped to his feet and began to protest that Edith was innocent, and should be shown leniency. Mr Justice Shearman showed none, he sentenced them both to death.

The public now felt sorry for Edith, they believed handsome young Freddy, they trusted him when he said that Edith was innocent, and a campaign was immediately launched to win Edith a reprieve. Over a million people signed a petition to Home Secretary William Bridgeman, asking for Edith to have her sentenced reduced. Bridgeman ignored the pleas and turned down Edith's appeal. Edith had become a shadow of her former vivacious self, she was hardly eating and seemed drained of energy. When the news came that her appeal had been declined, she went into raging hysterics. On Tuesday the 9th of January 1923 both Edith and Freddy were due to be executed. Edith was so hysterical she had to be drugged up with enough sedatives to fell a small horse, yet she still whimpered and cried. No one really believed she was to be hung, the belief in Holloway Prison was that Edith would receive a last-minute reprieve. A woman had not been hung for sixteen years, the British judiciary didn't make a habit of executing the fairer sex. Even the executioner John Ellis didn't believe he'd be hanging Edith that day. Yet, at the appointed hour, 9.00 a.m., Edith had to be carried from her cell, she was almost catatonic, yet still managing to wail like a banshee, screaming all the way to the execution room. A mile and a half across the city, in Pentonville Prison, Freddy Bywaters also made his way to the execution room, both lovers were executed simultaneously.

The story of Freddy Bywater's is tragic, yet no one argues that he was indeed a murderer, and under the law of the time had to be executed. Edith Thompson was a different story, there was no real evidence that she counselled Freddy into killing Percy Thompson, it was simply moral indignation that hung her. What was worst it was rumoured that Edith was pregnant at the time of her execution, despite hardly eating between her sentencing and execution her weight had gained considerably from 119lbs to 133lbs, rumours also circulated that Edith's insides had fallen out when she was hung, a possible euphemism for having miscarried perhaps. One thing is for certain after her execution, a discreet home office rule was passed stating that all women executed were to wear specially made leather panties.

Love destroyed Edith and Percy Thompson and Freddy Bywaters, love enraged their minds and drove them to actions they would not normally have considered. Love is a powerful motivator, it can act as a catalyst for both acts of wonder and destruction, it can be a saving grace or our greatest downfall. It intrigues us all, it enchants us, it pulls us towards it, telling us to ignore the danger sirens that screech in the back of our minds. The story of Edith Thompson and Freddy Bywaters shows that it's not only crazed maniacs who fall folly to the allure of murder to sate loves sexual ardours, but it could also be you or me if only for the turn of a pretty head and whispers of eternal desire.

An Affair Of The Mind

It's not often I feel sorry for a murderer, but in the case of Clifford Holmes, I find it hard not to. Holmes was a twenty-four-year-old soldier, he'd married young when he was only nineteen, and his wife, Irene, was only eighteen. He was a driver in the Royal Engineers and had seen active service in France, taking part in the bloody Dunkirk evacuations. These events and events he had witnessed in Palestine had obviously played on his mind and played no small part in the preface to the bloody murder of the woman he loved most in the world.

In January 1940 Holmes sent his wife, Irene, who was living in Manchester, England, a letter from the Gibraltar Barracks in Aldershot. The letter was vile, threatening and most of all, very disturbing. The letter accused Irene of committing sexual indiscretions, while Holmes had been off fighting for King and country. Irene concerned by the threatening tone of the letter took it around to a neighbour, who she knew was discreet and who had some experience in dealing with troubled individuals, this man was a Probation Officer by the name of Eugene Patrick Lee. Lee wrote to Holmes, admonishing him for his vile language and threats, but assured him that Irene was nothing but faithful to him while he was so dutifully serving his country at war. It seems Lee's assurances did no good, for in the next week two more vile and threatening letters arrived, each containing unfounded allegations of infidelity.

When Holmes was next on leave, Lee invited both he and Irene to his offices, where he commenced on some informal marriage guidance. This was after all the days when Probation Officers saw their remit as being to advise, assist and befriend those in society unlucky enough to need help and assistance. After giving the couple a crash course of counselling, where he believed he had patched up the differences between the unhappy pair, Holmes returned to Aldershot assuring Lee that his kind actions had achieved their desired goals and that he and Irene were now entering a new happier phase in their matrimonial ties.

On Monday the 26th of August 1940, Irene Holmes received another letter from Clifford Holmes, this was equally as vile as the ones she had received at the beginning of the year and continued to berate her in the most obscene terms for her adulterous behaviour, while Holmes was off risking his life. Irene took the letter around to Eugene Lee, who in turn advised Irene that enough really was enough and that she should seriously consider a separation order. Irene broken-heartedly agreed, the letters had become so violently threatening she was by now in genuine fear of what Holmes might do to her should he return from the Aldershot barracks. Irene also wasted little time after receiving this new letter, in leaving the family home she had previously shared with Clifford Holmes, and she moved discreetly into lodgings at 450 Stockport Road, Longsight. Holmes, receiving the news that Irene now desired a separation from him, went straight to Major Basil Charlton Deacon, his commanding officer, and asked for a spell of compassionate leave, in the hope that he might salvage his marriage. Major Deacon being sensitive to the fact that the war was shattering enough families, duly granted the request, and Holmes travelled back to Manchester, where he found the family home deserted.

On Tuesday the 8th of October 1940, Irene Holmes was granted her separation, on the grounds of Holmes' persistent cruelty. Clifford Holmes was furious, outside the court, he lambasted Irene, and informed her, "You won't get a penny out of me! I'll do you in first!"

Holmes refused to admit that his marriage was over, and he began to engage in behaviour which today we would recognise as those of an emotionally unstable stalker. By Wednesday the 9th of October 1940 Holmes had tracked down the secret address that Irene had moved to, he knocked on the door, dressed in his full military splendour, and informed one of Irene's fellow lodgers that he had left some important documentation in Irene's room. The lodger, Mary Jane Butler, told Holmes that Irene was out, but let him up to her room, where Holmes sat quietly for a while and, no doubt, he went through Irene's belongings, looking for evidence of the none existent affair he suspected his wife of having. Holmes had left before Irene returned, but later that evening Mary Jane Butler answered the front door of 450 Stockport Road to find Holmes stood on the doorstep once more, this time, dressed in civilian clothing. He barged past Miss Butler and made his way up to Irene's room, a blazing row erupted, and a few minutes later Miss Butler heard heavy footsteps running down the stairs, a few moments after that a distraught Irene entered Miss Butler's room, sporting a livid black-eye.

On Thursday the 10th of October 1940, Clifford Holmes spent the day going around the local pubs of the Greater Manchester area. At the Plymouth Arms, in Chorlton-Upon-Medlock, Holmes asked the barmaid, Mary Wilson, if he could leave his army kit behind the bar so that he wouldn't have to carry it around with him all day. Mary informed him he could leave everything but his rifle. Holmes remarked dejectedly, "That's what I wanted to get rid of, I might use it."

At 8.30 p.m. Mrs Florence Farrington answered a knock on the door of 450 Stockport Road, Holmes stood before her, rifle in hand. He barged passed her and marched determinedly up the stairs. Mrs Farrington followed and remonstrated with Holmes, who turned around and shouted into the frightened woman's face, "Mind your own business!" Holmes continued on his way, to Irene's room, and tried the handle to the door. Finding it locked, he called for Irene to open the door, but Irene shouted for him to go away. Upon this Holmes took his rifle and fired twice into the lock. Mrs Farrington ran for cover in Mary Jane Butler's room, and in the next few moments, five shots echoed through the house.

A few minutes later, Mary Jane Butler left her room and quietly made her way downstairs. In the back kitchen, Irene Holmes lay on a couch, Clifford Holmes leant over her as if in prayer, crying. The police were called for, as was a doctor, several of the residents knew the Holmes family, and so sent for Clifford Holmes' mother, a Mrs Snowball, who came to comfort her now inconsolable son. As Mrs Snowball entered the kitchen, Holmes looked up, and through tears, he spluttered, "Oh Ma, can you help her because I shot her." Holmes was cradling and rocking Irene's body to his chest, Mrs Snowball attempted to calm her son, by telling him that she believed Irene had just fainted. Holmes lay Irene back down but soon noticed that there was a large wound in her chest, over her heart. Holmes began to dig his fingers into this bullet hole, and Mrs Snowball solicited Holmes as to just what he was doing, to which he informed her he was, "Trying to get the bullet out which I have put there." His behaviour continued to deteriorate, and moments later, he was putting his hand up his dead wife's skirt and fondling her genitals. Mrs Snowball was obviously shocked by this peculiar and outrageous behaviour and begged Holmes to stop, Holmes became a little angry at his mother's protestations, and angrily spat at her, "I can love her, she's my own wife!" The anger soon dissipated, and Holmes was crying again within moments, weeping loudly, "Oh Irene, speak to me! I love you so!"

Not a moment too soon Constable Henry Fletcher arrived at the scene to take control, he was accompanied by a Dr Lenten. Irene had been shot five times, and stabbed, three times in the arm and twice in the stomach, using the bayonet that had been attached to Holmes' rifle. There was nothing the doctor could do, Irene was quite dead. As Constable Fletcher tried to lead Clifford Holmes from the scene, Holmes muttered dejectedly, "I have shot hundreds in France and Palestine, but had to miss myself." At first, this statement meant little to Constable Fletcher until he found a bullet on the floor of Irene's bedroom, a faulty bullet which had failed to fire. This bullet, Holmes informed him, had been intended to kill Holmes himself after he had murdered his wife. Holmes was then placed into the custody of Detective Inspector Robert Lennox, who formally charged Holmes with the murder of Irene Holmes.

Clifford Holmes trial for the murder of his wife commenced on Monday the 16th of December 1940, before Mr Justice Stable. The trial lasted two days, over which the whole sorry story of Clifford Holmes and his murderous paranoia was related to a gobsmacked court. Mr John Caterall Jolly and Mr Percy Butlin for the defence laid out the case that Holmes was not responsible for his actions, he was quite clearly mad. To this end, Major Purser of the Royal Army Medical Corp gave expert testimony that Holmes was suffering from the onset of schizophrenia, and therefore could not fully understand the implication of his actions when murdering his wife. Dr Walter Henry Grace, from the County Mental Hospital in Chester, had also examined Holmes, and in his expert medical opinion, Holmes was suffering from a sexual obsession which had brought on anxiety and neurosis. For the crown, the doctor of Strangeways Prison, Dr M. R. H Williams, who had no real expertise in mental illness, stated that he had interviewed Holmes five times while he was on remand and found him to be perfectly sane.

The jury went out on Wednesday the 18th of December 1940, they quickly returned, and in their brief absence had decided that they trusted the evidence of Dr Williams over the two expert witnesses, and therefore found Holmes Guilty of the cold-blooded, premeditated murder of his wife. Mr Justice Stable duly sentenced Holmes to death. There was one last hope, an appeal to the Home Secretary, Herbert Morrison. If Morrison reviewed the evidence and believed that Holmes was mentally unwell, then the execution could be averted. Morrison reassessed the evidence, and decided, like the jury, that Holmes was sane and in his own right mind when he murdered his wife. On Tuesday the 11th of February 1941, Clifford Holmes, damaged war hero, was executed for the murder of the wife he loved too much.

Intolerable Cruelty: Dr Geza and Hajna De Kaplany

I find Geza De Kaplany to be one of the most loathsome and odious men in the annals of crime. His actions almost above any others I find to be particularly cruel and detestable. A deliberately callous and spiteful crime committed out of sheer hatred and a desire to cause the woman he loved as much extreme physical pain as possible.

Born in Hungary in June 1926 into an aristocratic family, Geza De Kaplany had a strong religious upbringing, and a childhood spent pining after an absent mother who De Kaplany was said to have put on a pedestal and idolised. Conversely, he was brutalised by his father. On one occasion his father beat De Kaplany so badly he was permanently blinded in one eye. From that point on, De Kaplany wore tinted spectacles to hide the disability. De Kaplany spent much of his childhood being brought up by strict matriarchal governesses. His mother became a mysterious figure who he loved from afar and who took upon almost mythic qualities in his imagination as he spent less and less time with her. Some would later argue that within this childhood the seeds of a dangerous Oedipus complex were planted, which led to no other woman being able to meet the unobtainable standards of saintliness he bestowed upon his distant mother, and ultimately led to the horrid crime Dr De Kaplany committed. As a child, De Kaplany was taught that women fell into two distinct categories, good girls and bad girls. Good girls were religious and chaste and virtuous. Bad girls were loose with their morals and indulged in carefree acts of sexual pleasure. In 1942, De Kaplany had his first sexual encounter with a local girl. The peculiar moral standards that had been taught to the young man meant that he was deeply conflicted by the experience. He desperately wanted to enjoy the sexual act, but he believed that anyone who was willing to have sex with him so freely and casually must have been a "bad girl." Due to the moral conflict, this caused De Kaplany found himself unable to get an erection, and he henceforth became a figure of fun to the local girls.

This wasn't the only traumatic experience De Kaplany had during this adolescent period. Between 1939 and 1945 Europe was torn apart by war. Hungary was part of the Axis Powers, one of the countries who sided with Hitler's Germany. De Kaplany's three older brothers signed up to fight on behalf of the fascist ideology and were each killed during the various battles with Yugoslavia and Russia. By April 1945 Russia had swept into Hungary and captured the capital of Budapest. For the next forty-four years, Hungary would be a repressed communist state. It was a dark and dangerous period for anyone like De Kaplany, a keenly intelligent man with a deep intellect and aristocratic descent. His upbringing and social standing should have by rights made him diametrically opposed to the ideologies of his communist masters. The communist state feared such men as Dr De

Kaplany, and the AVH (the State Protection Authority, the Hungarian version of the KGB) executed 350,000 men and women and deported another 600,000 to the gulags, all because it saw intellectuals and former aristocrats as posing a threat to the state. De Kaplany avoided such a dreadful fate. Indeed, he seemed to prosper rather well under the Soviets. He attended the University of Szeged where he undertook his medical qualifications and eventually rose to the heights of a consultant cardiologist. De Kaplany probably kept his life by becoming an informer for the AVH, betraying his friends and aristocratic relatives for his own personal gain and to ensure his own safety. At least that's what some people believed. Kaplany himself would later put it about that he had played his part in the Hungarian Revolt of 1956. In fact, he told British authorities[iii] that he had been one of the architects and leaders of the revolt. However, others felt it deeply suspicious that he arrived in America at a time when Communist collaborators were being lynched on a daily basis in Hungary, and that he probably fled his motherland within days if not hours of the revolution breaking out. Some in the Californian Hungarian émigré community believed De Kaplany had feared the revolutionaries keeping hold of power, and had fled lest his collaboration with the communist regime come home to roost in a rather fatal way.

Upon arriving in Boston Dr De Kaplany became incensed that he wasn't immediately allowed to carry on working as a consultant cardiologist. His Hungarian qualifications were not recognised in America, and De Kaplany was forced to requalify, attending the prestigious Harvard University. De Kaplany wanted a quick fix, so rather than go through all the rigmarole of proving he could take on the complexities of heart surgery, he settled on a career as a consultant anaesthetist. It was said that he resented this downturn in his fortunes greatly, and was never truly happy in the role. He was apparently morose and constantly groused that such work was beneath his intellect and abilities. Despite his loathing for his lowly position, he obviously had a flair for anaesthetics, for in 1958 he gained himself a position as a lecturer of anesthesiology at Yale University. This teaching position didn't last very long, lecturing didn't hold the glamour of true medical work, and De Kaplany longed to be a dashing and admired consultant again. He eventually moved to San Jose where he took up a post as a consultant anaesthetist at San Jose Hospital.

In and around the San Jose Hospital Dr De Kaplany got himself quite the reputation for being a womaniser. He began by dating a nurse called Clara Gabriel. After just four dates, Dr De Kaplany asked for her hand in marriage, and Clara politely refused and subsequently distanced herself from the overly eager consultant anaesthetist. He then went out with a twenty-one-year-old receptionist at the hospital called Geraldine Smith. In April 1962, they went on a skiing holiday to Yosemite, where De Kaplany tried to inveigle his way into

Geraldine's bed. She refused the doctor's advances, and the next morning she discovered that Dr De Kaplany had gone home early in a snit. This left Geraldine stranded in Yosemite without the funds or means to get back home. After this disastrous enterprise Dr De Kaplany then dated a divorcee called Yvonne Sinonaglu, again Dr De Kaplany asked Sinonaglu to marry him, more than once, and each time she turned him down flat. She told him that the reason for her rejection of the proposals was the fact that she could not marry a Catholic. When De Kaplany got the hint, he moved on from Yvonne Sinonaglu and met a West German immigrant who took up a nursing post at San Jose Hospital, Margarathea Herbst. They dated for four months, De Kaplany proposed to Margarathea, and she accepted. It came as a total shock to Margarathea when De Kaplany told her in early August 1962 that the engagement was off, he was going to marry another woman. Now, only Margarathea Herbst became sexually intimate with Dr De Kaplany, but she would later testify that on the occasions when they did try to make love, he was usually plagued by chronic impotence. When he was capable of getting an erection, the lovemaking was brief and perfunctory. The great lady's man was all mouth and no trousers.

The other woman that Dr De Kaplany had cuckolded Margarathea Herbst for was a twenty-five-year-old beauty queen, model and exotic dancer called Hajna Piller. She was a Hungarian immigrant who had come to America with her parents when her father used the 1956 Olympics to defect to the west with the entirety of the Hungarian fencing team. Hajna really was strikingly beautiful, just the type of woman Dr De Kaplany felt he deserved. He made the initial enquiries about marriage not to Hajna directly, but to her mother, Illona Piller. The old lady was flattered by the suggested proposal, after all, who wouldn't want their daughter to marry into aristocratic stock? Especially when their family fortunes had sunk so low, their daughter had been forced to take up dancing in a seedy nightclub just so the family could make ends meet. Illona Piller made the relevant introduction and told her daughter in no uncertain terms that she should accept the immediate marriage proposal. Just three weeks after their first meeting, Dr Geza De Kaplany married Hajna Piller, and the couple moved into a spacious luxury apartment at 1135 Ranchero Way, San Jose.

Just days after returning from Honeymoon in Hawaii, a strain began to develop in the marriage. Dr De Kaplany became deeply suspicious of his wife's activities and began to obsess over the idea that she was unfaithful to him. Instead of joining Hajna as she sunbathed and lazed by the apartment's pool, Dr De Kaplany began to spy on her and obsessively watch her from their room, taking notes of who she talked to as she sat sun-worshipping. Instead of being happy with his beautiful new wife, De Kaplany became markedly sullen and introverted, and neighbours began to comment on the fact that he was quite clearly a jealous husband. It was also noted that there appeared to be little affection or physical contact between the pair.

Disaster struck when a friend of the De Kaplany's, a forty-year-old spinster called Jane Hajdu, told Dr De Kaplany that since their marriage Hajna had continued to sleep with one of her old boyfriends. Hajna had confessed to Jane Hajdu that since the marriage there had been little physical intimacy between the newly-weds, Geza De Kaplany had trouble getting and maintaining an erection. Hajna told Jane Hajdu that she was deeply fond of Geza De Kaplany, but she had needs which De Kaplany was incapable of satisfying. Jane Hajdu later testified that she had felt she was doing the right thing in telling Dr De Kaplany about the affair, that she was merely looking after the newly-wedded doctors best interests. Whatever her motivations, the next day Jane Hajdu took Dr De Kaplany to see divorce lawyer Scott Anderson. De Kaplany demanded that the lawyer start divorce proceedings immediately on the grounds of Hajna's infidelity, and he wasn't prepared to pay Hajna a penny in alimony. Anderson told De Kaplany that what he was asking was impossible. Dr De Kaplany would need far more evidence of adultery than the word of Jane Hajdu[iv]. Divorce was a long and expensive process, not only were their legal and court fees involved, Dr De Kaplany would have to pay for private investigators to discreetly follow Hajna and gather the evidence of her infidelity. Even then he'd definitely have to pay his wife alimony, nothing could prevent that eventuality. To Dr De Kaplany, this was unacceptable, and he decided to end the marriage in his own horrific way.

Just five weeks after the wedding between Geza and Hajna, on Tuesday the 28th of August 1962, an oppressive heatwave hit San Jose. Hospital staff were surprised to find the usually elegantly dressed Dr De Kaplany hanging around the hospital on his day off, wearing a pair of Bermuda shorts, a short-sleeved t-shirt and a pair of flip-flops. He made excuses for his presence at the hospital and was seen bobbing in and out various storerooms, loitering with suspicious intent. At 8.00 p.m. that evening, neighbours enjoying the evening sun witnessed Hajna arrive home, Dr De Kaplany opened the door to her, and she entered without showing her husband any physical affection. At 8.30 p.m. a neighbour knocked on De Kaplany's door to ask them if they would like to join the poolside party for cocktails. Dr De Kaplany answered the door dressed only in his Bermuda shorts, and he appeared "bewildered." He curtly announced that he was very busy, and rudely slammed the door in the neighbour's face. A few minutes later, classical music could be heard coming loudly from De Kaplany's apartment. In the apartment directly below the De Kaplany's, schoolteachers Jacqueline Behney and Nancy Helfrick started to hear more than just the music, they began to hear what they took for a series of screams followed by an incessant moaning and groaning sound which then steadily rose again to a constant agonised screaming.

At 10.11 p.m. the San Jose Police Department received a telephone call, all that the operator could hear was classical music played at a deafening level and what the operator took to be screams. The caller promptly hung up. Two minutes later they called again, this time the music was lowered, but the screams could still be heard in the background. "Send the police," a voice said, "I've hurt my wife. I've hurt her bad. She may die." A squad car was duly dispatched to apartment 30 at 1135 Ranchero Way, it arrived at 10. 18 p.m. There was a gaggle of residents outside on the patio waiting for the police, all of the apartment blocks residents had been disturbed by the frightful screams coming from the De Kaplany's apartment. The two officers made their way to apartment 30 and knocked on the door. A few moments later the door was opened by Dr Geza De Kaplany he was drenched in sweat and wearing his Bermuda shorts, a plastic apron and a pair of surgical gloves. "Come in," De Kaplany announced, "She's in there." Officer Jim Moir led the way into the bedroom, there was a horrible acrid smell in the air, chemicals mixed with what smelt like burnt flesh. On the floor between a pair of twin beds was Hajna, tied to the bed legs by her wrists and ankles with an electrical flex and surgical tape. Dr De Kaplany had used a surgical scalpel to make small incisions into Hajna's face shoulders, chest, and on and around her breasts and genitals, he had then used surgical swabs to daub undiluted nitric acid into the open wounds. Hajna had third-degree acid burns covering forty per cent of her body. The acid had effectively melted away Hajna's face, blinding her in one eye, and almost obliterated her right nipple and clitoris. It had also left her in unimaginable pain. Next to the body was a handwritten note, it was written in Hungarian and when translated read:

IF YOU WANT TO LIVE:

1) DO NOT SHOUT

2) DO WHAT I TELL YOU.

IF NOT YOU WILL DIE!

As Jim Moir frantically telephoned for an ambulance, Dr De Kaplany calmly stripped, took a shower and changed into a suit and tie ready for his inevitable arrest.

When interviewed Dr De Kaplany stated that Hajna only had herself to blame for what had happened. He had initiated sexual intercourse, only he'd been unable to gain, and erection and Hajna had ridiculed him for his sexual failure. He had then confronted his wife with his knowledge about her affair. She had admitted it, and told De Kaplany that her boyfriend was a much better lover than him. This had pushed Dr De Kaplany over the edge. *"I did it to take her beauty away from her,"* He explained casually, *"I did it to frighten her, to put the fear into her against being an adulteress."* The police charged Dr De Kaplany with Attempted Murder and Assault with a

Deadly Weapon and sent him to the County Jail to await trial.

On Sunday the 30th of September 1962, thirty-three days after the horrific act of torture, Hajna De Kaplany died from her injuries. Given the almost constant agony she had been in since her ordeal by acid, it was a mercy. The whole of California was appalled by the crime. Reporter Carl Sifakis called the murder, *"the most horrendous single murder in American history."* The District Attorney immediately substituted the existing charges for one of First Degree Murder and told the press that he would be seeking the harshest sentence available, execution in the gas chamber. Upon hearing the news, Dr De Kaplany collapsed to his knees, cradled his head in his arms, and as he rocked slowly backwards and forwards sobbing he kept repeating, *"Don't let them hurt me! Don't let them hurt me!"*

De Kaplany's lawyer, Edward F. De Vilbiss, felt that the best way of helping his client was to try and persuade a jury that De Kaplany was Not Guilty Through Reason of Insanity. De Kaplany point blank refused to accept this. He had not intended to kill Hajna. If he hadn't intended to kill her, it wasn't murder. He'd only wanted to take away her beauty and womanliness, the sexual allure that had caused her to be unfaithful. Anyway, it was his wife who was entirely to blame for her own death. She had driven him to it by mocking his libido and inability to make love to her, any reasonable man would have acted the same given the heinous provocation. De Kaplany was adamant that he would be pleading Not Guilty. The trial began on Monday the 14th of January 1963 before Judge Raymond G. Callaghan, and it was an utter sensation, in no small part due to the antics of Dr De Kaplany. On the second day of the trial, De Kaplany argued desperately that a photograph of Hajna De Kaplany's horrific injuries should not be shown to the jury. De Kaplany began to act like a client from hell. He talked over the prosecutors and even his own defence as they mitigated, and he began wildly shouting out instructions to his lawyers when they needed none. It was a simple legal argument that should have taken a few minutes, but Dr De Kaplany's antics meant it dragged on for several hours. When the judge finally and exasperatedly ruled that the photo was admissible as evidence and could be shown the jury, De Kaplany immediately jumped to his feet ran over to the photograph, and staring down at it, he grabbed dramatically hold of his head and began screaming *"No! No! What did you do to her? What did you do?"* De Kaplany had to then be physically restrained. The next day Dr De Kaplany came morosely into the courtroom and asked to change his plea to one of Not Guilty Through Reason of Insanity. When asked by the judge if he understood what he was doing, he pointed his finger at the photograph that had so upset him the previous day, and melodramatically replied, *"I am a doctor, and if I have done this then I must be mad!"*

Six psychiatrists examined Dr De Kaplany in order to establish his mental state. Three of the psychiatrists, Dr Johnsen, Dr Rappaport and Dr Shoor, all agreed that De Kaplany was perfectly sane at the time of committing the offence and therefore should be found guilty of murder. Three others, Dr Zaslow, Dr Beaton and Dr Lee disagreed. Dr Zaslow felt De Kaplany was, "*Severely disturbed*" and displayed "*impairment of conceptual thinking and use of proper judgment.*" Dr Lindsey E. Beaton stated that De Kaplany was, "*Very seriously ill, psychiatrically, psychologically,*" and that he was, "*Not able rationally, logically and consciously to govern his actions.*" Dr Beaton concluded that Dr De Kaplany's condition was probably compounded by his mother being a "*feminine ideal*" which had caused De Kaplany to "*somewhat reject women.*" Ah, the age of old dichotomy of a mummy's boy placing mummy so high upon a pedestal other women are unable to reach such dizzying heights of perfection, and hatred and resentment of anyone who attempted to even try. Dr De Kaplany took umbrage with this diagnosis and kicked up a right old stink in the courtroom as Dr Beaton elucidated his theory to the jury. In conclusion, Dr Beaton stated that he felt Dr De Kaplany was a paranoid schizophrenic. Dr Russell Lee had the most dramatic testimony of all the doctors. He revealed that he had been able to get hold of Dr De Kaplany's medical records from Hungry, no small feat during the height of the cold war, and these showed that Dr De Kaplany had been hospitalised in a *"neuropsychiatric institution"* in 1946. Further, Dr Lee stated that Dr De Kaplany suffered from multiple personality syndrome. Since 1956 Dr De Kaplany had been sharing his body with an overly macho Frenchman called Pierre La Roche who had latent homosexual tendencies. Pierre La Roche had been a ferocious womaniser in order to compensate for his homosexual feelings and had even fathered a child with a German immigrant called Ruth Krueger. Krueger had fled America back to Germany with La Roche's child in fear of De Kaplany/La Roche. After Dr Lee's testimony,

District Attorney John Schatz amazingly was able to track Ruth Krueger down. He had Ms Krueger flown back to America where she took the stand. She refuted that she had been in an intimate relationship with Pierre La Roche, her affair had been with Dr Geza De Kaplany. De Kaplany had never referred to himself as Pierre La Roche at any time during their relationship and had never made any intimation that he was French. She did, however, confirm that she had fathered De Kaplany's lovechild, a boy called Andreas. When Ms Krueger had told De Kaplany about the pregnancy, De Kaplany had told her that he was already married (he was not at the time) and that his wife was incarcerated in an insane asylum, and therefore he could not divorce her. De Kaplany told Ms Krueger that he would always provide for her and the child, and took out a large insurance premium which Ms Krueger would be the beneficiary of. Ms Krueger had not fled America, De Kaplany had persuaded her to leave using the insurance policy as a sweetener. Within hours of Ms Krueger having boarded the plane, De Kaplany changed the policy so that Ms Krueger and his unborn child would no longer be the beneficiaries. Instead, De Kaplany's mother was to reap the benefits of the insurance policy. Ms Krueger had been left trapped back in Germany with a child to support and no money to return to America and make De Kaplany face his parental responsibilities. Why had Dr De Kaplany acted in such a cruel and callous way towards Ruth Krueger? Well, put quite simply she was too plainer looking girl for Dr De Kaplany to even consider marrying. He believed that someone with his aristocratic genes deserved a stunningly attractive wife, not a Plain Jane.

The jury eventually retired on Monday the 21st of January 1963, they deliberated for over nineteen hours. When they returned, they stated that they believed Dr De Kaplany had been sane at the time of the murder and so was Guilty of Hajna's murder. However, although not legally insane they felt De Kaplany had quite clearly been mentally unwell, and so they recommended a sentence of life imprison instead of the sought after death penalty. This caused outrage in San Jose, the people wanted Dr De Kaplany to be gassed for what he had done, in no small part the anger was caused by the photographs of Hajna's horrific injuries. One juror even had to have police protection after receiving death threats. The public was eventually reassured by the authorities when they released a statement saying that due to the particularly cruel and gruesome nature of his crime, Dr Geza De Kaplany would be classified a "special interest prisoner" and would never be granted parole. The public was satisfied, and Dr De Kaplany disappeared into the penal system.

In 1975 Dr De Kaplany became eligible for parole for the first time. His parole board hearing was headed by Raymond Procunier, the chairman of the California State Parole Authority. Procunier made a rather curious decision before the hearing, he decided to remove all the photographs of his victim's injuries from De Kaplany's file and forgot to mention that De Kaplany was a "special interest prisoner," whose parole should be turned down flat. Without the pictures, the parole board could not put the injuries into context. They couldn't see the true horror of what De Kaplany had done. De Kaplany came across as just another man full of remorse who had committed a horrid crime of passion when mentally unwell. Heavily influenced by Procunier, the board unbelievably granted the barmy doctor parole. A few weeks after his being quietly released Geza De Kaplany applied to the parole board for special permission to fly to Taiwan where he wanted to become a missionary doctor. Again, unbelievably, Pocunier granted De Kaplany permission to travel to Lutsao. De Kaplany practised medicine in Taiwan for the next four years, becoming a cardiologist again, he even remarried. In 1979 De Kaplany tired of the constant checks he was required to go through as part of his parole conditions and disappeared, fleeing Taiwan with his wife. Interpol was informed, and an international arrest warrant was issued. When the public discovered that the hated Dr De Kaplany had not only been given parole after just twelve years but had also been allowed to leave the country so he could continue practising medicine, there was a public explosion of rage and condemnation. Raymond Procunier took the full blame for De Kaplany's release and disappearance and was forced to resign. Although he stated his resignation was for "personal reasons" no one was left in any doubt it was due to his peculiar handling of the De Kaplany affair.

It seemed that the American authorities felt that De Kaplany was more trouble than he was worth, they really didn't want the hassle or cost of having to bring him back to America and re-imprisoning him. Several times the American authorities received firm tip-offs of where Dr De Kaplany was living, they even once found out that Interpol was just hours away from arresting him, and so his local American Embassy telephoned De Kaplany to warn him. If this wasn't all extraordinary enough, the American Army actually employed Dr De Kaplany, giving him a job as a doctor in a health clinic on an army base in Grafenwöhr, Bavaria. This all seems rather extraordinary, and some have wondered why Dr De Kaplany was given such exceptional treatment? Well, some have argued that after fleeing Hungary Dr De Kaplany became an asset for both British Intelligence (his having fled Hungary via the United Kingdom) and the CIA. That perhaps his predilection for spying and tittle-tattling on his friends continued upon his reaching America, and he passed valuable information on possibly dangerous communist spies in the Hungarian émigré community onto the American authorities. From this, it's further postulated that when he went on the run from Interpol, the American intelligence agencies turned Dr De Kaplany back into an asset. They then planted Dr De Kaplany in locations where he could worm his way into communities the intelligence agencies had concerns about, and Dr De Kaplany reported back like a good little tattle-tale. This is all speculation, but it's certainly food for thought given the exceptional way he was treated by the American authorities when by rights he was on the run from them. Eventually, however, Dr De Kaplany became a naturalised German citizen, he moved to the town of Bad Zwischenahn, where the elderly and retired doctor and possible spy lives to this very day.

The Paraquat In The Pie

Susan Barber began her relationship with Michael Barber with a lie. Deceitful seventeen-year-old Susan tricked Twenty-four-year-old Michael into believing that her daughter was the result of their young carnal desires, all the while she knew full well that the child was the product of an ill-planned fumble with her ex-boyfriend. Yet, Michael believed Susan, and the couple married in 1970 when the little girl he mistook for his daughter was just six months old. Michael and Susan lived the kind of domestic life many married couples find themselves trapped in after a few years of marriage, the passion was dead, and they were stuck in a rut. Susan was a housewife, looking after the three children, while Michael went out to work in a local cigarette factory. Their social life consisted of going to their local pub, The Plough, where Michael played the sport of none sportsmen, darts. Here Susan would keep the scores and was regularly mocked by the locals for her terrible grasp of sums.

Richard Collins was twenty-three, handsome and what the women amongst you might describe as quite the dish. He was a neighbour of the Barbers, he drank in the Plough, he joined the darts team with Michael, and he and Michael began to go on fishing trips together, and when Michael was in work, Collins began to share an interest in Michael's wife. Susan accepted Collins advances with alacrity. She longed for the naughty and spicy sex that had long since waned and died in her relationship with poor old Michael. The affair began when Susan asked Collins to come around while Michael Barber was at work, there was an emergency, the fridge had broken down, and she didn't want the food in there to spoil[1]. When Collins arrived with his box of tools, the scene played out like something from a bad pornographic

---

[1] Some sources state that the affair began much earlier when Collins was only fifteen years old, if this is true then Susan Barber should also be considered not only a murderess but a predatory paedophile.

movie, with Susan seducing the bemused and then delighted young man. The affair continued for some time behind Michael's back, he had no idea that his good friend and wife were deceiving him in the most hurtful and intimate of ways.

At 4.00 a.m. on Saturday the 31st of March 1981 Michael left the Barber home at 29 Osborne Road, Westcliffe-On-Sea, Essex. He was going on a fishing trip which would last until late the following evening. Collins had been due to join Michael on the fishing trip but had cried off sick. So, Michael went on his merry way alone, and as soon as he had turned out of the street, Collins left his home dashed up the road and joined Susan for what they hoped would be an eighteen-hour marathon session of rumpy-pumpy. The sexual frolics began in the living room, with clothes and underwear being stripped and discarded, leaving a sexual breadcrumb trail through the house to the bedroom. Unfortunately for them all, Michael Barber had got to the Thames Estuary and found the conditions unconducive to fishing, there was a high wind and a light fog, so Michael dejectedly turned around and went back to 29 Osborne Road. He opened the front door and in a bemused state found the clothes leading their sexy trail up the stairs, he followed them all the way to his bedroom, where, with horror, he found his best friend locked in a sexual frenzy with his wife. Michael went into a black rage, Collins raced passed Michael and down the stairs in an attempt to escape from the house. Collins then struggled with the Yale lock on the front door, and Michael caught up with Collins as he tried to escape into the front garden. Susan Barber joined the fray, pulling Michael off Collins and opening the door to aid her lovers escape. Michael turned to Susan and gave her a thick ear, sending her sprawling to the floor, he then turned and chased Collins down the garden path. Collins' vaulted over the garden fence like a prized hurdler and ran naked up the road to the safety of his own house. By now, it was early morning, and several people in the neighbourhood were up and on their way to work, several neighbours witnessed the embarrassing events, and the affair became the talk of the neighbourhood. Not only that, but Michael Barber also returned to his home and gave Susan a terrible beating for her infidelity. The beating was so severe she was forced to go to the doctors to have the livid wounds seen too. The terrible retribution that Michael Barber had inflicted upon his wife wasn't enough to deter her from her illicit affair, oh no. The very next day, as soon as Michael was off to work, Susan telephoned Collins and invited him back into her marital bed.

The couple brooded on the terrible beating Michael had given to Susan, and together they decided that if the affair was to continue, they had to do something to protect Susan. Rather than be a little more careful and engage in sexual activities away from Susan's marital home, the pair decided that the safest course of action was to murder Michael Barber. Susan took herself off to

Michael's potting shed and retrieved some weed killer, Gramoxone. This contained the unusual and deadly active ingredient of paraquat.

On Thursday the 4th of June 1981, Susan Barber cooked for Michael's dinner a steak and kidney pie that was laced with paraquat. Michael woofed it down, unknowing that he was sealing his own deadly fate. Paraquat attacks the lungs, making it difficult for the victim to breathe, it also corrodes the throat. On Friday the 5th of June 1981, Michael Barber began to feel the immediate effects of the poison, a headache, which caused him to go to the company matron. Soon after he was vomiting, and sent to see his GP. Here he was prescribed antibiotics and linctus. The medicines didn't help. Soon Michael was having severe difficulty breathing and was experiencing prickling pains in his throat and chest. One night, just before bed, Michael collapsed onto the bathroom floor, and he was rushed to hospital in an ambulance. Initially, Michael was diagnosed with pneumonia but failed to respond to treatment, on top of this, his kidneys began to fail. Doctors observing Michael began to suspect it could be paraquat poisoning, due to its distinctive symptoms, and so sent some blood off for tests. Good fortune was on Susan Barber's side, the test results were mixed up in the laboratory, and they came back negative. When the doctors treating Michael tried to double-check the results, the laboratory lied to them to cover up their mistake. Misinformed, doctors began to treat Michael for the extremely rare Goodpasture's Disease, an anti-immune condition where the body's own immune system attacks the lungs and kidneys, causing them to collapse and fail. He was transferred to the Hammersmith Hospital in London, where it was felt he could be better treated for such a rare and dangerous disease. When Michael failed to respond to treatment for Goodpasture's Disease, it left doctors completely baffled and helpless to save him. On Saturday the 27th of June 1981 Michael Barber died, the flummoxed doctors apologetically put his death down as renal failure and pneumonia.

Susan Barber believed she had got away with murder, she had Michael Barber cremated as soon as she could to destroy the incriminating evidence. With indecent haste on Friday the 3rd of July 1981, his body was cremated at Southend Crematorium, it had been less than a week after Michael's death. That night the merry widow moved Richard Collins into her dead husband's bed before his ashes had even cooled. The honeymoon for the murderous mistress and her lover lasted less than six weeks. Susan grew bored with Collins, now there was no longer the spicy frisson of danger to the relationship she found it just as suffocating and boring as her marriage had been. She chucked Collins out of 29 Osborne Road and left him to go slithering back to his cuckolded wife. Susan Barber then wasted no time in moving another lover into her home, a man who she had only recently met in The Plough. Martin Harvey was a man of only twenty, a big barely steelworker with massive hands and an even larger sexual appetite.

Unbeknown to Susan Barber, before she could burn away all the evidence two very keen pathologists had carried out an autopsy on Michael Barber, given the peculiar symptoms of his death. Professor David Evans and Dr Peter O'Brien were aware that early tests had ruled out paraquat poisoning, but they were not too sure. All the evidence they could see in the body pointed to just such a conclusion. So they preserved all the major organs in formalin and sent them off to the National Poisons Unit for testing. Or at least they thought they had, at this point, another cock-up arose, and the organs were never sent, they just remained in a bucket in a cupboard at the mortuary. After several months Professor Evans went like a bull in a china shop through the Hammersmith Hospital, demanding to know where his test results were.

He uncovered the mistakes that had occurred during the original lab test that had led to the deadly misdiagnosis and the second mistake that had led to the failure of the organs to be sent off to the National Poisons Unit. This time taking no chances, Professor Evans sent the samples, not to the hospital laboratory, but off to ICI, the manufacturers of paraquat. ICI tested the organs and confirmed what had been so painfully obvious to Professor Evans and Dr O'Brien, Michael Barber had died of paraquat poisoning. By now it had been nearly nine months since Michael Barber's death, and the Hammersmith Hospital was forced to send an apologetic letter to the Southend Coroner and the Essex Police informing them that the hospital had ballsed-up. It now did, in fact, look like Michael Barber had died in some very suspicious circumstances indeed.

As these dramatic events unfolded, Susan Barber had begun living a life even emperor Caligula might think was a bit sexually excessive. She had received Michael's death grant from his employers, a sum of just over £2300, and bought herself a Citizen Band Radio. With this, Susan gave herself the moniker "Nympho," and took to the airways inviting lonely truckers to 29 Osborne Road for carefree nights of frolicking fun. Once she had lured a man into bed with her, she would turn on the radio and broadcast her pants and moans and ecstatic cries of pleasure for all lonely truckers to hear. Detective Chief Inspector John Clarion was the only cloud on the horizon, the one man who could blot out Susan's desire of discovering her own personal sexual nirvana. On Monday the 5th of April 1982, Clarion arrested Susan Barber at her home, and Collins at the warehouse where he worked. Collins was the first to break, he told Clarion how he and Susan Barber had openly discussed murdering Michael Barber, how Susan had asked Collins to knobble the breaks on Michael Barber's car so that Michael would hopefully die in a fatal car accident. Collins had refused this suggestion, pointing out that even a cursory examination of the car's engine would lead to the crime being discovered. That's when Susan had remembered the particularly lethal poison that Michael had acquired during his short-lived career as a gardener. It was still in the potting shed. Collins had watched as Susan had poured the poison out, and was well aware of the purpose for which she intended to use it. He'd also been present when the doctors at Hammersmith Hospital had first suggested to Susan that Michael may have been suffering from paraquat poisoning and had watched on later that evening as Susan Barber had poured the remainder of the incriminating substance down the kitchen sink.

On Monday the 1st of November 1982, Susan Barber and Richard Collins appeared at Chelmsford Crown Court, charged with murder and conspiracy to murder respectively. Susan Barber pleaded not guilty, it was her contention that she had never intended to kill her husband, simply to, "make him suffer as I have suffered." Even to the most warm-hearted of juries Susan Barber's cold-hearted actions in the immediate wake of her husband's death, taking her deceased husband's best friend into her marital bed before her husband's body was cold, played heavily against her. Even the vocal feminist movement who usually stand up for the rights of battered wives (as Susan Barber undoubtedly was) to protect themselves from violent, thuggish husbands, could find little to empathise with in Susan Barber's case, given her selfish sex-obsessed and callous actions. Inevitably Susan Barber was found guilty of murdering Michael Barber, and as he sentenced her to life imprisonment, Mr Justice Wolfe commented on Susan Barber's method of murder, "I cannot think of a more evil way of disposing of a human being." As for her spurned lover, Richard Collins was found guilty of conspiracy to murder and was given the unbelievably light sentence of only two years imprisonment.

A World-Class Conman: Carol and Charles Stuart

Carol and Charles Stuart were an attractive couple. Both were thirty-years-old, Charles or "Chuck" to his friends was particularly handsome, square-jawed, tall, dark-haired, classically handsome in a rugged matinee idol way. He looked sporty, and indeed he helped to coach the local little league team in the upmarket Reading district of Boston. Carol was tall, slim, dark-haired and had a mouth of pearly white shining teeth that lit up her face whenever she smiled. It was the late 1980's, and both were what would have been termed Yuppies, or Young Upwardly Mobile Professionals. They were an affluent couple, they could afford a good car, a nice house and mobile phones when such things were the exclusive domain of the gauche and wealthy. They were also well off enough to take out life insurance policies on each other. Something which would lead to a deadly folly.

Charles and Carol had been married for four years. Now, I said before they were affluent, they were, but it was Carol who brought home the bacon. Charles worked for an upmarket furriers called Kakas and Sons who were based in Newbury Street in the city of Boston, and Carol was an attorney who specialised in tax law. In the eights, where greed was good, and people weren't so squeamish about wearing animal furs Charles and Carol raked in the money. Not that Charles always played it fair, he was known to lie in order to get the edge over people. He'd lied to Carol and her family about his education, telling them he'd got into college on a football scholarship, he hadn't, in fact, he'd barely scraped through high school and dropped out of community college after less than one semester. That's why compared to his wife he wasn't doing so well in life, Charles was after all a glorified store manager, if for a very high-class shop. It might have been a very exclusive store with a very large paycheque, but it still left a bitter taste in Charles' mouth that his wife was the principal breadwinner in the family. That was another thing about Charles, he was a bit old fashioned, and secretly held some very outdated and outmoded views about women and their place in the world. He was also secretly racist, not that he'd let any of his upwardly mobile friends know this, but his racist views would play a major part in the subsequent crime.

The Stuarts were about to start a family, Carol was pregnant, and their future looked very rosy indeed. The only problem was Charles Stuart didn't really want children. He was worried a child would eat into his expendable income, and he wouldn't be able to do all the nice things he liked to do with his money and spare time. Charles liked to dress in thousand-dollar suits, and eat at fancy restaurants and drive around in fancy cars. Such a lifestyle didn't come cheap. What if Carol got used to life on easy street, just sitting at home all day looking after the baby? What if they were left as a one-income family? What if it was left to him to do all the "real work," while his wife just loafed about? Then Carol started to state in no uncertain terms that they had to move to a bigger house to accommodate the new baby. Who would have to pay for this? Carol certainly wouldn't while she was off work caring for the newborn baby, no, it was just more of Charles hard-earned money being wasted on something he didn't want. He asked Carol if she would get an abortion, and she point blanked refused. Carol came from a large Italian family, and that's just what she wanted for herself, she didn't want just one child, she wanted to have as many as she could during her childbearing years. So, Charles sulked. He complained to his friends that his perfect and well-balanced life was about to be ruined, and he began to plot a way out of both fatherhood and his marriage.

On the evening of Monday the 23rd of October 1989, Charles and Carol were returning home from an antenatal class at the Brigham and Woman's Hospital. Charles drove the car into the Roxbury district of Boston, into the Mission Hill area, where something terrible happened. After driving aimlessly around for some time, he told Carol he was lost, and pretending that he was trying to get his bearings, he pulled over on a deserted side street off St Alphonsus Street, called Horadan Way. Here Charles removed a gun from a gym bag he had placed in the backseat, and he shot Carol at point-blank range in the back of the head. He then turned the gun on himself, shooting himself in the stomach. Bleeding profusely Charles used the Carphone to dial 911 and tell the emergency services that he and his wife had been shot in a carjacking. For thirteen minutes Charles was on the phone with the dispatcher, determinedly telling the man at the other end of the line that he did not know where he was, and could not see any useful reference points to guide the police or ambulances. The dispatch operator scrambled a squad of police cars and an ambulance to go to Roxbury and search the area for Charles and Carol. Only when Charles was sure that Carol was dead, did he give the operator enough information to ensure the police and ambulance would arrive in time to save his own life.

As Charles was taken covered in blood from the car, he was asked by a police officer who had shot them. Charles said it had been a failed carjacking and he had been shot by a black man with a raspy voice, wearing a black tracksuit with three red stripes down the arm. The ambulance crew worked on Carol as they drove her back to the hospital where less than an hour before she'd attended the antenatal class. It was quite clear she wouldn't survive, but they hoped they could save the baby. Upon reaching the hospital, baby Christopher was delivered by caesarian, he was two months premature, and unfortunately, both mother and baby died. Charles was rushed into emergency surgery, and for a while, it looked touch and go as to whether he would survive.

You see somehow Charles had bungled his own shooting and had inflicted quite a serious wound upon himself. This did at least give the story of a carjacking greater verisimilitude, but it also left Charles needing a colostomy bag.

Now the police were impressed by what information Charles Stuart gave them, as one senior officer put it, *"He gave police officers quite a lot of information about what had transpired, I was quite impressed how much detail and how much recall he had, considering what he'd been through."* Boston in the 1980s was a hotbed of racial tensions, some of the city's police officers were terribly racist, and a pregnant white woman being shot by a black man was all the excuse some officers needed to get very heavy-handed in the predominantly black neighbourhood of Roxbury. An extra one hundred police officers were immediately poured into the neighbourhood to search for the alleged gunman. This action immediately aggravated the racial tensions in the community and nearly brought

Roxbury to a riot. Even today people in Roxbury refer to this time as *"the reign of terror"* of Boston Police in the neighbourhood, and many still remember and are willing to talk about how being black and walking through the streets of Roxbury was to risk harassment from the police. Many young men were put through humiliating strip searches at the side of the road or had the police smash up their homes as they undertook fruitless searches as part of the Stuart investigation. Many asked if the police would have put so much effort into finding the killer if the victims had been black. Probably not was the considered answer. Indeed, the very same night that Carol Stuart was murdered, a young black man had also been shot dead just two blocks away, yet this murder received no media coverage, and the police seemed to do very little to find his killer.

As police investigated, they heard a rumour that a fifteen-year-old street hoodlum had been bragging about shooting the Stuarts. The police spoke to this young man, and he quickly changed his story. He hadn't shot the Stuart's, but his uncle had. The uncle was a thirty-nine-year-old man called Willie Bennett, a known offender with a long antecedent history, he had previous for robbery, drugs offences, violence, and gun offences. The police arrested Bennett and immediately put him in a police line-up. Charles Stuart unhesitatingly picked Bennett out as the man who had shot him and his wife. Willie Bennett found himself being charged with murder. The case against Bennett was far from watertight, however. The police raided the house Bennett shared with his grandmother, they failed to find the gun used in the crime, they failed to find the tracksuit Charles Stuart had described, they failed to find any of the jewellery or wedding rings taken in the alleged robbery. Nevertheless, the police were convinced that Willie Bennett was responsible for the murder, and focused in on him to the exclusion of all other possibilities.

With the police focusing on Willie Bennett, they were a little surprised when one of Charles Stuarts' best friends came forward with new information. David McClean told the police that Charles Stuart had approached him to illicit assistance in the murder of Carol. Charles had told McClean that he was unhappy wasting his life as a salesperson in a shop, he wanted to open his own restaurant, but Carol was unwilling to let him take the financial risk. The only way Charles could fulfil his dream was if Carol was out of the way, and then use the money from the life insurance policy he had taken out on Carol to pay for his new business venture. McClean was appalled by the notion and told Charles in no uncertain terms that he would not be helping to murder Carol Stuart under any circumstances, let alone when she was heavily pregnant. Concerned by how badly David McClean had reacted, and fearing his friend would go to the police, Charles tried to backtrack and make out that it had been a desperately unfunny joke. Of course, he had no desire to murder his wife, he'd been pulling McClean's leg. It seems that McClean had been satisfied with this explanation, but as soon as news of Carol's murder hit the headlines, his old suspicions returned, and McClean went straight to the police. The police pushed this information to one side, so focused were they on the black suspect, Willie Bennett. David McClean went away feeling very angry that the police weren't taking him or his story seriously.

The police were forced to take David McClean's story seriously when Charles' own brother came forward to support it. Matthew Stuart was Charles younger and less successful brother. He was twenty-three, and in dire financial straits, he'd never really got his house in order and was stuck earning minimum wage, was drowning in debt, and had begun dabbling in drugs. Charles had told Matthew that he would give him $10,000 if he helped Charles with a simple insurance scam. Charles was going to set up a carjacking, and all Matthew had to do was dispose of some jewellery that would be allegedly taken in the fake incident. Charles agreed readily. Only he hadn't realised that the insurance money Charles had spoken about was the $100,000 life insurance policy on Carol's life. Matthew told the police that he had arrived at the scene of the shooting to find Carol fatally wounded, and his brother in a serious state from the self-inflicted gunshot wound to the stomach. Charles had hastily stuck a bag in Matthew's hand which contained the gun Charles had used to murder his wife, along with what little valuables and cash they had had on them that night, including their wedding rings. In a panic, Matthew had taken the bag and thrown it off of the Pine River Bridge in Revere. If the police held any scepticism about this story, it abated when Matthew took them to the spot where he had dropped the package, and in the mud and silt below the bridge, they recovered some of the allegedly stolen items and the murder weapon.

The police had no option but to turn their attention from Willie Bennett and look a little closer at Charles Stuart and his possible motivations for wanting his wife dead. When they re-examined Stuart more closely, they discovered that despite the added inconvenience of a colostomy bag, he was living it up good style. He'd received his £100,000 insurance money and was now spending it like money was going out of fashion. The police also became aware of a beautiful young college graduate called Debra Allen who it appeared had turned Charles Stuart's head just prior to his wife's untimely demise. Ms Allen had come to work at Kakas and Sons as an office clerk, and Charles had struck up an instant friendship with the attractive young woman, a friendship that everyone could see was rather intense shall we say. Now, Ms Allen has denied that their relationship was anything other than a platonic friendship, but the police were able to prove that there were an awful lot of phone calls going on between the pair just before and immediately after Carol's death. The rather intense friendship does seem to prove that Charles Stuart was willing to have his head turned at least, and was possibly trying to line up the next Mrs Stuart ready for when he was young free and single again. Indeed, the staff at Boston General Hospital were very upset at how Charles had conducted himself in the immediate aftermath of his wife's death, especially when Ms Allen came to visit. Their behaviour towards one another was said to have been far too familiar and affectionate. Charles was, in their opinion, hardly the grieving widow.

On Wednesday the 3rd of January 1990 Charles Stuart learnt that his brother had turned him in. Charles went to see the family lawyer. The lawyer told Charles that there was nothing he could do, he would need a criminal lawyer and a damned good one at that. Charles fled, he booked himself into the Sheraton Motel in Braintree, and here he sat in room number 231 and brooded. Charles could see no way out of the situation other than spending the rest of his life in prison. Before going to bed that night, he asked the motel staff for a 4.30 a.m. wake-up call. In the early hours of the next morning, Charles showered and dressed and left the motel. He got into his brand new Nissan Maxima, and he drove to the lower deck of the Tobin Bridge. Here Charles pulled the car over to the side of the road and put the hazard lights on. He placed his driving licence on the passenger seat and then wrote a hasty suicide note, *"My life has been nothing but a battle for the last four months. Whatever this new accusation is, it has beaten me. I've been sapped of my strength."* Charles Stuart then stepped out of his car, walked over to the barrier and threw himself over the edge to fall the two hundred-eighty feet and drown in the freezing waters of the Mystic River.

In the immediate aftermath of Charles Stuart's suicide, there was a lot of finger-pointing and accusations fired around as to who was to blame for falling for his ridiculous story. The Boston Globe called Charles Stuart *"a world-class conman,"* he wasn't. His crime played on the racist attitudes and beliefs of a police force who were willing to believe that a black man was more likely to murder a pregnant white woman than her seemingly law-abiding white husband. The press, in turn, felt guilty for believing Charles Stuart and giving their sympathy and support and turning the whole event into a sickening media circus where even the broadsheets like the Boston Globe began to act like a seedy tabloid newspaper. The supporting characters in the whole tragedy fared no better. Matthew Stuart had taken a plea deal, he pled guilty to Conspiracy to Defraud and Possession of a Firearm and received seven years imprisonment. Upon his release Matthew sunk further into his drug dependency, he died of a drugs overdose in 2011 at the age of just forty-five in a homeless shelter in Cambridge, Massachusetts. The DiMaiti family, the family of Carol Stuart, sued Edward F. Kakas, the owner of Kakas and Sons, for wrongful death. It transpired that Charles

Stuart had taken the weapon used to kill Carol from the premises of Kakas and Sons, where the owners had failed to secure the weapon properly. The company claimed they had forgotten they even owned the gun or that it was kept on the premises. It was rather telling that Kakas and Sons didn't even realise that the gun was missing until after Charles Stuart had killed himself, and the police traced the weapon back to their store. The DiMaiti family also acknowledged the harm and upset that had been caused in the Roxbury and Mission Hill areas of Boston in the wake of Carol's murder. The DiMaiti's set up the Carol Stuart Memorial Scholarship which offers school scholarships to promising students who otherwise wouldn't get the opportunity to go to college because of the deprivation in the Mission Hill area. So far, the scholarship has helped over 250 young people from Roxbury and Mission Hill to pay for their college education at a cost of $1.5 million to the DiMaiti family.

Soon after being cleared of murdering Carol Stuart, Willie Bennett was arrested for an armed robbery on a Brookline video store. He was tried and found guilty of this offence, and subsequently served ten years imprisonment. Bennett always maintained his innocence about this crime. He stated that he was set up, and it was the police's revenge after he had so publically embarrassed them when he proved not to be the murderer of Carol Stuart, "*I felt they always wanted to get me for something,*" he complained bitterly years later. Bennett sued three of the police officers who had worked on the Carol Stuart murder case. Bennett alleged that the officers had attempted to coerce and bully, threaten and frighten associates into making incriminating witness statements against him. The case was eventually thrown out of Court in 1995. Bennett blamed the police for his mother's early death, and his grandmother having a heart attack and a stroke on the very night the police raided his home looking for the elusive evidence that sat under the Pine River Bridge. Bennett remains bitter towards the

Boston police force to this day, *"I have no faith in law enforcement... Nothing has changed. You still have those same racist cops on the police force."*

The actions of Charles Stuart had ripples which he could never have foreseen. Not only did he murder his wife and unborn child, but he also ruined the lives of his own brother and the Bennett family. He exposed the racism which was lying under the surface of the Boston Police Force and forced that organisation to re-examine its approach to race relations, and it's dealing with the poor and predominantly black areas of the city. It has been argued by some that the Boston Police Force now has some of the best race relations compared to other cities in America and that statistically black people are far less likely to be shot by a Police Officer in Boston than anywhere else. The murder of Carol Stuart also forced the media, most notably the Boston Herald and Boston Globe, to ask how they could have been so fooled by the handsome and conniving killer, and caused damage to their esteemed reputations as reputable purveyors of the news. Where its reporters being inadvertently racist in believing Charles Stuart? Did the way they gleefully and unquestionably report the arrest and persecution of Willie Bennett say something about barely repressed racist attitudes in the media? Charles Stuart could never have foreseen how his callous actions could have affected the children whose lives were immeasurably improved by the scholarships they were awarded by his wife's memorial foundation. We should not see this as Charles Stuart's legacy, however. This is the legacy of his wife, Carol. She was a woman who wanted nothing more than to be a mother to as many children as she could, and who in death is helping to improve the lives of disadvantaged children to this day.

Never Can Say Goodbye

"If people say to you or suggest that what we have witnessed was just a tale of lust, they are ignorant fools. If people say this was just an ordinary boyfriend-girlfriend falling-out, are they not blind?" - Stephen Coward QC during the trial of John Tanner.

The murder of Rachel McLean by John Tanner is one of the most callous, cold and calculating acts of deceitfulness and brutality in the annals of crime. John Tanner coldly and methodically went about his life in the wake of the murder, deliberately building up what he believed was a cast-iron act of blasé innocence. Yet he had already been condemned as a liar by the words of his victim in her secret diary.

Rachel Margaret McLean was a strong-willed and intelligent girl who had a brilliant future ahead of her. She came from a small and tight-knit family, her father was an engineer for British Aerospace, her mother was head of languages at the local school in Poulton, near Blackpool, England, and she had two younger brothers who idolised her as she went off to study English literature at the prestigious Oxford University. If Rachel had made the break to university afresh, as many do, leaving behind loves young dream to pursue the sexual opportunities of a new town far away from her families prying eyes, then perhaps Rachel would be alive today. Unfortunately, as it was, Rachel made the decision to stay in a long-distance relationship with her possessive boyfriend, John Tanner.

John Tanner was older than Rachel, he was twenty-two, yet despite his older age, he was deeply emotionally immature and lacking in self-confidence. He was originally from Whanganui in New Zealand, but he had moved to England in 1986, to study Classics at Nottingham University. By 1990 Tanner had made his way to Blackpool, where he began to make friends with people on the periphery of Rachel's social circles. Rachel was only eighteen when she met Tanner. It was at a party at her then boyfriend's house. Soon afterwards Rachel had ended that relationship, and a chance meeting with Tanner at the Adam and Eve nightclub in Blackpool, where he was a glass collector, led to Rachel inviting Tanner to her nineteenth birthday party. It was at this party that Rachel and Tanner began their sexually charged relationship.

On Saturday the 13th of April 1991, Rachel and Tanner had become engaged[2], to the outside world it seemed like the perfect relationship, yet privately Rachel was beginning to have doubts about Tanner, one could even

---

[2] Rachel and Tanner had originally become engaged on Valentine's day 1991, but Rachel had second thoughts overnight and the very next days she had talked Tanner out of the accepted proposal.

say she was beginning to loathe him. She wrote damningly in her diary of her relationship with the immature Kiwi:

"What is truly cancerous is his self-pity and the vampire-like way he leeches on my affection. Will I marry him; will I get engaged to him, simply because I cannot be bothered to make the effort to stop it?"

What had gone wrong with the initially sexually thrilling relationship? Well, it was the age-old story, Tanner had become obsessive and controlling. He demanded that Rachel come to visit him every weekend in Nottingham, where he had moved back to. He began to demand blow by blow accounts of everything Rachel had done while she had not been with him, who she had met and what she had talked about. He would phone Rachel's student accommodation at 25 Argyle Street, Oxford, at random times throughout the week, and if Rachel wasn't there, and she couldn't explain her absence, then there would be hell to pay. When Tanner was admitted into a hospital for a minor operation, which Tanner was erroneously obsessed with being to remove a cancerous growth, he demanded that Rachel drop all her important studies, move to Nottingham, and nursemaid him through his recovery. Tanner was turning into a particularly pernicious poster-boy for domestic abuse.

On Thursday the 11th of April 1991, John Tanner arrived at 25 Argyle Street, to visit Rachel for the weekend. Over the course of the four days Tanner stayed, he proposed to Rachel once again, she again agreed to marry him. Tanner left Argyle Street on Monday the 15th of April, he alleged that it was on the train home to Nottingham that he wrote a letter to Rachel, which read in part:

"My Dearest lovely Rachel, Thank you for such a wonderful weekend... I love you now and forever."

Over the next week, Tanner called Rachel several times, only to be told by her increasingly concerned housemate, Victoria Clare, that she had not seen Rachel for several days, and that she didn't know where Rachel was. Tanner began to show signs of concern, on Thursday the 18th of April 1991 Tanner wrote Rachel a further letter, in this missive he wrote:

"Being without you is a terrible burden to bear, but I live in the knowledge that I shall be in your arms next weekend. I miss you."

On Friday the 19th of April 1991, Rachel missed an appointment with her personal tutor, to discuss her assignments and oncoming exams. College authorities contacted the McLean family to ask if Rachel had returned home to Blackpool, the McLean's, in turn, informed the college that they had not seen or spoken to Rachel for some weeks. Now alerted to Rachel's disappearance, the college authorities reported her missing to the police on Saturday the 20th of April 1991. As a week had already passed since the last sighting of Rachel, the details of the case were quickly passed onto the Criminal Investigation Department. A description of Rachel was given to all local police officers, and a search of 25 Argyle Street was carried out. During this search, the police discovered Rachel's diary, and inside they read her dark and disturbing concerns about her boyfriend. As a result, Tanner was interviewed by Detective Superintendent John Bound. Tanner seemed overly eager to tell the detective about how sexually exciting the relationship was, and how on his visit to see Rachel between Thursday the 11th of April and Monday the 15th of April 1991, they had made love at least ten times. He explained to Bound how on Monday the 15th he and Rachel had travelled to Oxford Train Station by bus, here while waiting for Tanner's train for Nottingham to arrive,

Rachel had met a friend from university. Tanner described this man as looking like a "rock fan" with long greasy brown hair, a thin, sallow complexion and ripped jean. He had been told the man's name but could not remember it. Tanner claimed the trio had sat and shared coffee together in a cafe, as the man had agreed to give Rachel a lift home once Tanner was safely ensconced upon the train. Bound immediately felt that this statement was untrue, he had already read Rachel's diary and understood how possessive Tanner was, he immediately recognised that Tanner would never have let Rachel go off with another man, even if it was only for an innocent ride home in his car.

Bound brought Tanner to Oxford, where he made him take part in a press conference. Here Tanner asked the public to help the police, "out of sheer consideration for her mother and father and myself." He then took part in a reconstruction of his last alleged movements with Rachel at Oxford Train Station. Despite himself, Tanner seemed to enjoy the attention and appeared to like getting to grips with PC Helen Kay as he re-enacted his last kiss with Rachel on the station platform. Tanner then helped the police to construct a photofit of the "rocker" Rachel had gone off with. The resulting picture held an eerie similarity to Tanner himself.

As this media circus played out, the police carried on with the very serious business of searching for Rachel, the river Cherwell was dragged, local scrubland was searched, sewers and cesspits were investigated. After the reconstruction, witnesses came forward, one had read the reports of Tanner having shared a cup of coffee with the young man Rachel had allegedly subsequently gone off with. This lady had seen Tanner sat in the coffee shop at Oxford Train Station, but importantly he had been alone, he had also been writing a letter, probably the letter he claimed to have written on the train back to Nottingham. The police then went to the local bus company, they knew exactly what bus-stop Tanner had alleged he and Rachel had boarded the bus at, and at what time, Tanner had stated they had travelled on the 5.00 p.m. bus that went to Oxford Train Station. Luckily for the police, an onboard computer kept a record of how many tickets were given out at each stop, this proved that Tanner had boarded the bus alone. Witnesses were tracked down who had also travelled on this bus, and they confirmed that Tanner had been all by himself.

Unable to find Rachel's body, Superintendent Bound consulted Oxford County Council to ask if they had plans of 25 Argyle Street, Bound wanted to see if the original search had missed anything, a basement or some such hidden area. The hunch paid off, Bound discovered that the house was "underpinned," in other words, the foundations had been deepened to strengthen them, and as a result, there were large cavities under the floor of the property. On Thursday the 2nd of May 1991, in a cupboard under the stairs, the police discovered such a cavity. Tanner had squeezed himself into this gap pulling Rachel's semi-dressed body after him. He had then dragged the body under the house, under the hallway, into the small recess under the floorboards of Rachel's bedroom, where he had left her body. The weather had been so mild decomposition had been minimal, and so no telltale smell of death had been detected by Victoria Clare. Within an hour of the discovery, Superintendent Bound ordered the arrest of John Tanner.

Tanner remained calm under questioning for several hours. Then, finally, in a police cell, he broke down into tears. He asked to speak with Detective Sergeant Mike Scarlett, and under caution he began his statement with the words, "I wanted to see you, to say sorry because of all the lies I have told you." Tanner stated that on the night of Sunday the 14th of April 1991, Rachel had told Tanner that she felt the relationship was taking over her life, she was sinking into depression because of his possessiveness, that getting engage had been a mistake, and she wanted to end their torrid affair. Tanner tried to change Rachel's mind, Rachel in response told Tanner that she was certain the relationship was over because she had found herself being unfaithful to him on two occasions. Tanner claimed that upon hearing this a blazing row had erupted, Rachel had gone to slap him, and at this point, he had snapped, he strangled Rachel, but he couldn't exactly remember the details, he was suffering from the convenient temporary amnesia encountered by a lot of killers. Naturally, there were some inconsistencies in Tanner's story, it appeared that Tanner had stopped trying to manually strangle Rachel, and as he moved away, Rachel had rolled over onto her stomach, perhaps to seek to crawl away from the murderous assault. Tanner had then wrapped a tea-towel around Rachel's neck and continued to strangle her with the ligature from behind. In her desperation, Rachel had pulled out clumps of her own hair, which were found still grasped under her fingertips. Tanner was unable to remember this break in the murderous attack, possibly because it proved he had time to compose himself and think better of his actions as he went off to get the tea-towel, yet he still chose to continue with his diabolical deed. Rachel had soiled herself during the attack, and Tanner had bathed and reclothed her body, before lying Rachel's lifeless corpse on her bed overnight, while he slept sobbing on the floor. Tanner finished his confession with the self-piteous words, "I cannot understand how I managed to destroy the thing I hold dearest."

Tanner's trial began at Birmingham Crown Court on Monday the 2nd of December 1991. Tanner pleaded not guilty to murder, but guilty to manslaughter on the grounds of provocation. It was a terribly cowardly defence, in a snide way Tanner was blaming Rachel for her own murder. To this end, Stephen Coward QC for the defence tried to make Rachel look like a manipulative and two-faced girl, who publicly besotted and beguiled the hapless Tanner like the biblical Delilah, while privately pouring scorn and humiliation on him in her diaries. Coward compared the words of a valentine's card Rachel wrote to Tanner which read in part:

"To my John the fulfilment of my heart and my mind's desire... You are and will always be my Valentine, and I am yours forever."

Yet, that same night in her diary Rachel had written about Tanner:

"You sick childish bastard. You are so busy generating self-pity... I hope your romance (with yourself) lasts forever and ever."

Coward was keen to show that Rachel was very aware how she was deceiving the man counsel was now trying to make out was a poor unsuspecting dupe, a man who the cold and callous Rachel had been toying with the affections of. Coward read to the jury an extract from Rachel's diary where she talked about her deception of

Tanner's affections, and how easy she found it to be so two-faced to him:

"The way the mask slips on so easily to protect him from my naked soul."

When Tanner took to the witness box, he cried and bemoaned his lot. When asked by Coward about why he had set about the elaborate lies after Rachel's murder, Tanner replied that it had not been a deliberate subterfuge. He, in his own mind, refused to admit that he had murdered his "beloved" Rachel. He had simply carried on in a manner in which he believed he would have lived his life if Rachel really had disappeared. To Tanner, his words and actions were not an elaborate lie. In his mind, he had created an elaborate fantasy, and so he was from that point on recounting what he really believed happened, after persuading himself it was the truth in his own shocked and befuddled mind. In Tanner's own words, "I could not accept I had killed my love, I lived in a world of pseudo-reality which was based on the reality I had known until the point I killed her. I encapsulated myself in a false world." This was why Tanner had taken such pains to hide the body, telling his counsel, "If there was not a body to be seen, I could more easily convince myself nothing had happened." Yet Tanner continued to show a lack of empathy for what he had done and the propensity for self-pity which Rachel had so abhorred in him. This was encapsulated when he highlighted to Coward how since the murder, Rachel's actions had continued to blight his life, 'Life is lonely, sir. It's lonely because I have lost the ability to trust people'. He then went on to decry, "I do not believe Miss McLean actually sought to destroy me, although the circumstances have proved to be so." Of course, Stephen Coward helped Tanner along in his attempts to appear to be the hard done by and lovesick fool. Coward said of Tanner's murderous actions in his summing up, "(It) was not the act of a sick psychopath who got a kick out of killing beautiful girls, nor that of a cold and calculating killer. It was a love story, a grand passion...

their intense love was greater than most people ever know, and such an intense affair does not fit with a cold, calculating killer."

On Thursday the 5th of December 1991 the jury retired to consider its verdict. They deliberated for four and a quarter hours, it seems that Tanner's story and the twisting of Rachel McLean's character by Coward had been somewhat persuasive, for the jury came back with a ten to two majority verdict, Tanner was guilty of murder. Three of the jury were in tears as Tanner was sentenced to life imprisonment for the brutal killing of Rachel McLean. Mr Justice Kennedy acknowledged to the twelve jurors that the case had been emotionally difficult for all concerned, "It has been a particularly burdensome one for you," he was at pains to concede.

As Tanner began his life sentence, it was reported that he began to dwell on the alleged affairs that Rachel had admitted to having before her murder. His cellmate reported that Tanner began to hate Rachel, and actively blame her for provoking her own murder and his subsequent incarceration, a continuation of the self-piteous behaviour he had displayed throughout their relationship. Despite the unusually cold and calculating facets of the crime, Tanner served only eleven years and eight months in prison, hardly the life sentence Rachel's family were promised Tanner would serve. In 2003 he was released from prison and promptly and quietly extradited back to New Zealand.

The Deal With The Devil

'In the unremittingly bleak and featureless prairie that is her mind, she has always been a special little girl... It was not that her conscious was clear, it was that she never had one'. – Christie Blatchford on Karla Homolka.

How far would you go for the one you loved? Would you lie for them? Would you steal for them? Would you sexually assault and kill for them? I would be really rather worried if you answered yes to that last one, but frighteningly, there are those who would have to say yes, because they have committed the ultimate taboo to keep their love. Karla Homolka did some terrifyingly sadistic and peculiar things to keep her man happy, that man was Paul Bernardo, a sadistic and cowardly rapist. Yet on the surface, the incredibly beautiful couple had a seemingly perfect life that led to the press dubbing them The Ken and Barbie Killers.

Karla Leanne Homolka was born on Monday the 4th of May 1970, in Port Credit, St Catherine's, Ontario, Canada. She was born into a loving and close-knit family. She was the older sibling to two sisters who adored and looked up to her, Lori and Tammy. Her parents Karel and Dorothy were lower-middle class and were able to give their children a comfortable upbringing. Karla was also lucky enough to be born with two attributes which saw her excel at the Sir Winston Churchill Secondary School, she was pretty, and she was smart. She also had a love of animals which led to her working in a veterinary surgery and aspire to possibly train at some point to become a vet. It was this love of animals that put her on a path that changed her life and led to the murder of two innocent teenagers and her own unsuspecting sister.

Paul Bernardo was altogether a different animal, born on Thursday the 27th of August 1964, in Scarborough, Toronto. He came from an abusive home, where the man he believed was his father, Kenneth, would regularly beat his mother, Marilyn. I said the man Paul Bernardo believed was his father, you see things were so bad for Mr and Mrs Bernardo even before Paul Bernardo was born, Marilyn found succour in the arms of her first love, and the dalliance led to her impregnation. Kenneth Bernardo was a sexual pervert, he had convictions for sexual assault on a minor and engaged in peeping tom activities before he later graduated to systematically abusing Paul Bernardo's younger sister. The physical and emotional abuse endured by Marilyn Bernardo caused her to suffer a complete mental breakdown, she was unable to complete the simplest of household duties, and Kenneth Bernardo took to keeping his now grotesquely overweight wife locked in the cellar, like some hideous monster from a Victorian gothic horror story. One would have thought that the trauma of growing up in such a dysfunctional household would have caused Paul Bernardo to become introverted and sullen, but he didn't. He learnt how he could cleverly manipulate the people around him so that they would like him, and therefore wouldn't hurt him. A defence mechanism created by a lonely and scared little boy, which would ultimately help to turn him into a cold-blooded killer. In his late teens, Paul Bernardo began to invest his money in motivational books such as "How To Win Friends and Influence People." He began to watch television evangelists and emulate their sense of style, their confidence, their easy-going manner of talking and their body language, developing a new persona of a cool and smooth man in control of any given situation. After graduating high school and taking up a part-time job as a salesman, he went to the University of Toronto to study accountancy, just like his so-called father. Bernardo was studious during the daytime, attending classes and completing his assignments, of an evening, he would cruise the bars of Toronto and pick up women, take them back to his dorm, where he would subject them to painful acts of sodomy. Upon his graduation, he gained employment at Price Waterhouse Accountants. All the while, he cultivated his modern libertine image, dating multiple women, many at the same time, smooth-talking and manipulating them so that they didn't seem to mind his wandering libido. Each of his girlfriends reported the same disturbing behavioural traits, Bernardo was controlling and enjoyed rough and painful sex which centred around the anus. Several of these women had to threaten police action when Paul harassed them after the breakdown of their relationships. Paul was evidently becoming a man who didn't take rejection or the word "no" easily.

On Saturday the 17th of October 1987, Karla Homolka's love of animals began to lead her down a dark road. She attended a conference with her friend Debbie Purdie, on the riveting subject of pet food, held at the Howard

Johnson Hotel in Toronto. After the conference, Karla and Debbie went for a meal in the hotel's bar, as they ate, in walked Paul Bernardo. Debbie Purdie described the meeting between Karla and Bernardo as love at first sight. She said there was a palpable "electricity" in the air as they first met. Within a few short hours of that first meeting, Paul Bernardo was checking him and Karla into a hotel room for an all-night sex session. Karla was only seventeen, yet already she was sexually experienced enough to please Bernardo a great deal. Bernardo was obviously as smitten with Karla as Karla was with Bernardo, for he asked for Karla's telephone number, something he rarely did to one of his random pickups. It was the start of a bloody and murderous relationship.

From the outset, not everything was perfect in the relationship, not that Karla seemed to mind, but Paul Bernardo began to act like his father, in a controlling and abusive manner. Within a matter of months, he was completely controlling Karla Homolka's life, he would tell her what to wear, and make her change her clothes if he did not like what she had chosen to put on herself. He ordered her to have her hair styled in a certain way. He began to monitor and control the foods she ate if Karla put on a pound in weight Paul Bernardo would be displeased, and he would call Karla fat and ugly. Bernardo even made Karla keep notes on his decidedly ropey motivational techniques, "remember your stupid, remember your ugly, remember your fat." Not only did Bernardo personally drum this tosh into Karla's head, but he also made her write down this sickening mantra and repeat it over and over when he wasn't present. Alongside this, he made Karla write reminders on how she should behave, not to talk back to Bernardo, and that if he asked for anything, Karla should supply it "quickly and happily." Then the sex between Bernardo and Karla began to take decidedly dark overtones. Bernardo began to make Karla wear a dog's collar and leash to bed, which he could either choke Karla with or lead her around the bedroom on all fours like some submissive animal. He began to ask Karla to masturbate in front of him for his voyeuristic pleasure. At first, he was happy to simply watch Karla alone on her bed, probing her genitals gently with her fingers, until Bernardo became bored with the timidity of these acts. He then began to ask Karla to use implements, to insert roughly inside her, objects such as wine bottles. During the act of full-on intercourse, he started to use sexually humiliating language, hurling foul four-letter insults at Karla in his sexual rage, names such as "slut" escalated to "bitch" and finally to the ultimate sexual insult, when he called her a "cunt." After this, during what could no longer be termed as the act of lovemaking, but only as degrading sexual acts, Bernardo started to show how he liked to have true power over his girlfriends. One night Bernardo wrapped a wire cord around Karla's neck and nearly choked her to death. Outside of the bedroom things were getting no better, in fact, they were taking a decidedly sinister turn for the macabre. Bernardo took an instant liking to Karla's fifteen-year-old sister, Tammy. He began to pay the young girl attention, give her compliments. Tammy started to see Bernardo as a protective older brother. Then one night during sex, Bernardo suggested a little role play. Not the harmless fun of one or other partner pretending to be a police officer or fireman or air hostess, no, Paul Bernardo wanted Karla Homolka to pretend to be her underage sister, with Bernardo taking on the role of the suave seducer taking Tammy's virginity. Bernardo even followed in his father's footsteps, carrying out sinister peeping tom behaviour, peering through Tammy's bedroom window, watching her undress, all the while Tammy was blissfully unaware that Bernardo was stood only feet away masturbating.

With Karla so besotted with Bernardo, he quickly realised that he could get the immature young woman to do whatever he wanted, as long as she believed that she might lose his love. So, Bernardo began to make a fuss about Karla not having been a virgin when they first made love. Over the course of several weeks, Bernardo built agony upon agony over this. He turned Karla's previous sexual encounters into a major disruptive factor in their relationship, something that was threatening to destroy their life and happiness together. Then Bernardo offered Karla an out, he could forgive Karla her past sexual indiscretions, if he was allowed to take her younger sisters virginity. Now, most of us would be appalled at such a suggestion and would tell the sleazy, morally, and sexually bankrupt individual to take a hike. Karla Homolka was so besotted with Paul Bernardo, she felt that his defiling her fifteen-year-old sister was a small price to pay to keep his love. Of course, Tammy Homolka would never agree to take part in a perverse sexual act with her sister's boyfriend. Tammy was too wholesome and chaste for that. So Bernardo and Karla came up with a plan. By now Karla worked as a nurse in a veterinary surgery, where she could easily procure halothane, a drug used to sedate and anaesthetize animals during operations. On Sunday the 23rd of December 1990, during a pre-Christmas family get-together, Bernardo and Karla brought their vile plan to bitter fruition. They began to drug Tammy's drinks with halothane, they even put some in her spaghetti bolognese. She passed out on the settee, as her mother, father, Bernardo, Karla and her sister, Lori, sat watching Christmas television. When the remainder of the family went to bed, Bernardo carried Tammy down to the basement, Karla placed a rag soaked in halothane over Tammy's nose and mouth, and Bernardo raped Tammy as Karla Homolka looked on, videotaping the whole vile act. When Bernardo had finished defiling the unconscious teen, he cajoled Karla Homolka into sexually assaulting her own sister. As Karla carried out the twisted sexual acts, Tammy vomited, as she lay on her back, she began to choke on the vomit. Bernardo and Karla panicked, they couldn't revive Tammy, despite amateurish attempts to give her CPR. With Tammy dead the deviant couple acted calmly and rationally, they redressed Tammy's corpse, carried her upstairs and lay her on the settee, they hid all evidence of the halothane and the video of the rape, and then called for an ambulance. If Bernardo and Karla were worried about being caught, they never showed it. Everyone believed their story of it being a tragic case of a young girl drinking too much alcohol over Christmas and choking on her vomit as she slept. Indeed there seemed to be physical evidence to back this story up, a burn mark on Tammy's cheek caused by the Halothane was mistaken for a carpet burn, created when Karla and Paul Bernardo allegedly attempted to give Tammy CPR. As Karla showed a public face of grief, privately she gloated over her sister's death. Paul Bernardo videotaped Karla talking about her sister's rape and murder, gushingly eulogising over how much she enjoyed the murderous experience. The couple then moved upstairs to Tammy's bedroom, Karla undressed, put on some of Tammy's clothes, and then the couple made love on the dead girl's bed. Happy Christmas Tammy Homolka, from your loving sister and future brother-in-law.

Three disparate events converged, leading to Paul Bernardo and Karla Homolka murdering their second victim. The first event occurred a full two weeks before the fateful night of the couple's second glut of violence. It was a tragic event that seemed unrelated to the disturbed couple's sordid sexual adventures, yet was intrinsically linked to them by the cruelty of fate. In the first week of June 1991, Burlington, Ontario, teenager Chris Evans died in a tragic car crash. Meanwhile, Paul Bernardo and Karla Homolka had moved into a property together, before their impending nuptials. Bernardo had decided that the household could do with some extra income to help the couple live in the lavish lifestyle they were becoming to love. To this end, Bernardo took to regularly crossing the Canadian/American border, buying cigarettes in bulk cheaply in America, then crossing back over to Canada and selling his ill-gotten gains, with a healthy markup of course, to his friends and colleagues. So that his car was not noticed regularly crossing the border on this small scale smuggling enterprise, Bernardo took to stealing number plates off of cars, which he then used to hide his own cars registration number. On one such thieving trip, he met fourteen-year-old Leslie Erin Mahaffy. The final incident that led to Leslie's murder was one that Leslie's parents regretted forevermore. Leslie was a bit of a tearaway, she had run away from home several times, and had the propensity to drink and take drugs. This was heartbreaking to her parents, who were sensible, caring folk, Leslie's mother was a teacher, and her father was an oceanographer. On Friday the 14th of June 1991, Lesley had been to the funeral of her friend, the late Chris Evans, after the funeral Lesley had gone with a large group of teenagers to sit off in a local wood, drink, smoke pot and remember the good times they'd had with Chris. Realising that this was an emotional event for their daughter, Debbie and Dan gave

Leslie the relatively late curfew time of 2.00 a.m. Despite such a late hour being given to the fifteen-year-old, Leslie still managed to break the curfew. To teach their wayward daughter a lesson, Debbie and Dan Mahaffy locked all the doors and windows to the family home, so that Leslie could not sneak in. This led to Leslie deciding not to knock her parents up and face their wrath yet again, but to dejectedly walk the streets, while she thought of a way of getting into the property. Paul Bernardo noticed Leslie as she wandered aimlessly around. He sneaked up on her and either, depending on which of the murderous couples account you believe, put a knife to her throat or wrapped a sweater tightly around her head. Paul Bernardo then guided the terrified young girl to his car and then drove her back to the couple's new home at 57 Bayview, Port Stanton, Ontario. Once back home, Bernardo began to show Leslie a little hospitality, although she was blindfolded he gave her a drink of champagne and a cigarette, he then disappeared upstairs to his bedroom, where he woke Karla. With

Karla awake, Bernardo began to video the whole horrid event. Twenty-four hours of agonising torture awaited the petrified girl. It began with Karla sexually assaulting Leslie, all under Bernardo's direction, with him instructing Karla exactly what to do, where to touch and titillate the terrified teen. When Karla had finished, Bernardo moved in, he savagely raped the girl, both anally and vaginally, all through the agonising experience Leslie was wide awake and screaming, unlike his previous victim, and this only seemed to heighten Paul Bernardo's pleasure. The couple had learnt their lesson, and after Tammy's death, Leslie had only been mildly sedated using the halothane. Once the Bernardo's had gorged themselves on their sordid sexual sickness, Paul Bernardo claims he attempted to take the very much alive Leslie home. He attempted to wake Leslie, who had fallen asleep so that he could guide her to his car, but he was unable to rouse her from unconsciousness. He tried his best, of course, to try and revive the girl, but his attempts at CPR failed. I personally don't believe this load of old tosh for a moment. The self-serving explanations the Bernardo's gave for the "accidental" deaths of their victims strike me as the same MacGuffins John Reginald Halliday Christie espoused half a century before when he desperately tried to wriggle his neck out of the hangman's noose. Also, this explanation does not explain how Leslie was very much conscious, if slightly woozy during the videoed portions of her terrifying ordeal. The Bernardo's in all probability deliberately murdered Leslie so that they didn't have to deal with the inconvenience of a living witness who might lead the police to the door of their new home. What happened next was truly sickening and showed the true contempt the Bernardo's held for their victims. On Father's Day, when Dan Mahaffy was worrying about the fate of his missing daughter, Paul Bernardo took Leslie's body into the basement and dissected Leslie into bits using a circular saw. He then encased her limbs into blocks of concrete, drove them to Lake Gibson, St Catherine, Ontario, and dumped them in the shallow waters of the lake. Just over a fortnight later on Saturday the 29th of June 1991, the very day Paul Bernardo and Karla Homolka got married, a fisherman returning home from a days' leisurely fishing trip found the first of the concrete slabs that parts of Leslie had been entombed within. Then a little later, Leslie's head and torso were found floating in the cold waters of the shallows. Suddenly the Ontario police realised the terrifying prospect that they had a particularly deranged killer on their hands.

The wedding of Paul Bernardo to Karla Homolka was a lavish fairytale affair, with a horse-drawn carriage, a $2000 wedding dress, an a la carte dinner menu which included pheasant stuffed with veal, and £50,000 worth of wedding presents. It was like a wedding out of a Disney film. Yet despite the fairytale air, Karla Homolka was acting more and more like the wicked stepmother, as opposed to the innocent princess. Her "wedding present" to Paul Bernardo was a particularly sordid one. She invited a local high school girl around to the couple's home, once alone on the premises with the under-aged girl, Karla plied her with drinks laced with halothane. The girl was nicely unconscious for when Bernardo came home from work. When he arrived, Karla invited Bernardo to rape the young teen. Just like with Tammy and Leslie, Bernardo then insisted that Karla also partook in the sordid sexual depravity. When Karla had sated her desires, Bernardo took over again, this time anally raping the poor girl. When the sexual frenzy was over, Karla took the still unconscious girl and placed her in bed for the night. The next morning the young girl awoke feeling immensely sick, and with no memory of the previous evening. The Bernardo's simply laughed this off, explaining to the inexperienced schoolgirl that it was all normal side effects of drinking too much alcohol. The girl never suspected a thing; that is until several years later when prosecutors tracked her down and apologetically informed her and her family that they had discovered footage of the rape in the Bernardo's sordid video collection.

Kristen Dawn French was another fifteen-year-old schoolgirl, she was popular, pretty, athletic, a medal-winning ice skater. On Thursday the 16th of April 1992, Kristen was crossing the parking lot of the Grace Lutheran Church in St Catherine's, Ontario. As she made her way across the car park, a pretty young blonde woman beckoned Kristen over to her car. The stunningly attractive blonde told Kristen she needed directions. As Kristen looked at the map and pointed out what the woman needed to do, a man came up behind her, stuck a knife to her throat, and ordered her into the back of the car. The Bernardo's had struck again. It was a sloppy kidnapping, carried out in broad daylight, with several helpless onlookers watching the sorry debacle. Nevertheless, the kidnapping was successful. The Bernardo's got Kristen back to their home, and over the next three days, they videotaped Kristen being subjected to some of the most humiliating and disgusting, vile and degrading acts a person could endure. Analingus, coprophilia, frotteurism, urolagnia were among just some of the horrendous and sadistic sexual acts the Bernardo's subjected Kristen too, as well as a torrent of verbal abuse and physical beatings. At first, Kristen was compliant and submissive, but as the brutality and sadism rose, she began to fight back, "I don't know how your wife can stand to be around you?" She spat with contempt at Bernardo at one point. When Paul Bernardo remonstrated with Kristen for her increasing none compliance and asked why she refused to engage willingly in some of the depraved acts of sexual madness, Kristen replied bitterly, "Some things are worth dying for." Kristen's death was not recorded on film, but the Bernardo's later stated that Kristen, when left alone for a few moments, attempted to escape from the Bernardo's hideous company. When Karla realised that their victim was escaping, she took after her with a mallet, bringing it down upon her head, felling Kristen to the ground. Karla then proceeded to finish the job off by garrotting Kristen to death. When the life was squeezed out of the teenage girl's body, Karla with blasé detachment went up to her bedroom and blow-dried her hair. On Thursday the 30th of April 1992, Kristen's naked body was found dumped like a discarded plaything in a ditch off a quiet backstreet.

Kristen French was mercifully the last victim of the Bernardo's, but what followed the murders was every bit as shocking as the Bernardo's sickening attempts to murderously spice up their relationship. A witness who saw the abduction of Kristen French believed that the car she had seen was a beige Camaro. Detectives paid for billboards to be put up around Ontario showing such a car, and asking locals with any information to come forward. Unfortunately, the witness was mistaken, the Bernardo's didn't own a beige Camaro, but a gold Nissan. After this lucky escape, their luck began to run out as another part of Paul Bernardo's seedy past came back to haunt him. Paul Bernardo was already well known in Canada for his criminal antics, it was not his real name that tripped so easily off the tongues of Ontario's scared residents, no, Paul Bernardo had become more popularly known as the Scarborough Rapist. Between May 1987 and May 1990, Bernardo had committed fifteen sexual offences, ranging from sexual assault and attempted rape to full-on penetrative rape. You might have realised that the Scarborough Rapist began his reign of sexual terror at roughly the same time that Paul Bernardo met Karla Homolka, and it has been suggested that Karla actively encouraged, cajoled and persuaded Bernardo to release his sexual demons on the wider public. Two of Bernardo's closest friends suspected Bernardo of being the Scarborough Rapist, and both independently told the police about their fears. As a result, Bernardo was interviewed by the Scarborough Police and submitted a DNA sample. The police found Bernardo to be polite and seemingly honest and helpful with his answers. Although he bore a striking resemblance to a composite sketch of the Scarborough Rapist, Bernardo was able to confidently persuade the police he was not the man they were looking for. His name was put low down on the list of suspects, and as a result, every time someone who seemed a more fitting suspect came along Bernardo's DNA was bumped further down the list of specimens to be tested. This proved very embarrassing for the police in the long run, as it meant that law enforcement agencies were in possession of the evidence that could have caught the rapist and stopped the Bernardo's killing spree before it had even begun. For two years, Paul Bernardo's DNA languished in a fridge waiting to be tested and declare loudly and publicly Bernardo's guilt. Two years the police deeply regret.

At home, things were getting fraught between the Bernardo's. The murders were beginning to play on

Karla's mind. She began to believe that the girls murdered in their house were haunting the property. She started imagining hearing bumps, bangs and the disembodied voices of her victims coming from the cellar, where the bodies had been hidden and dismembered. Karla went so far as to consult with a local psychic by the name of Lori Disenthio. As a result of this Karla carried out a DIY exorcism, pouring ammonia down the drains of her house, and commanding the trapped souls of her victims to head towards the light and leave her and Paul Bernardo in peace. Karla also took to carrying around an amethyst crystal in her pocket, to deflect any bad energy or evil vibes. On top of this madness, Paul Bernardo's sadistic tendencies were being held in check for shorter and shorter periods. On Sunday the 27th of December 1992 Bernardo's rage boiled over, and he beat Karla with a heavy rubber torch, so badly that he gave her two black eyes, severely bruised her arms and broke one of her ribs. When Karla's parents saw the injuries that Paul Bernardo had inflicted onto Karla, they forced her to go to the hospital, where naturally the police became involved. With the police involved, they persuaded Karla to leave Paul and to take refuge with relatives. Karla decided not to move in with her mother and father again but decided to go and live with an auntie and uncle. The uncle was a member of the Niagara Police Department, and over time he started to become suspicious of the things his niece was saying about the Scarborough Rapist, and the 'Green Ribbon' killer, as the press had dubbed the murderous couple. Karla's uncle also had his interest piqued by Karla's distinctive Micky Mouse watch, which seemed to be almost identical to one that Kristen French was known to wear, but which had been absent from her naked body.

Then events began to develop with lightning-quick speed. Bernardo's DNA was finally tested by the police forensic team and came up as a perfect match for the Scarborough Rapist. Suddenly the police realised that Paul Bernardo had been interviewed briefly for both the Scarborough

Rapes and the Green Ribbon killings. He'd been interviewed by police very briefly after Kristen French's murder. This had only been a formality because Bernardo's name had been linked to the Scarborough Rapes previously, and there had been allegations of rape and stalking by an ex-girlfriend. All local men who'd been accused of such crimes were now being tracked down and spoken to. At the time the police had been relatively satisfied that Bernardo had nothing whatsoever to do with either the Scarborough Rapes or the Green Ribbon killings, suddenly they couldn't be so sure, and the investigation began to look like it could explode out of all proportion. Indeed within just hours of the DNA test results becoming known, some police officers were telling their press sources, off the record, that the Scarborough Rapist and the Green Ribbon killer were one in the same person. Karla Bernardo was interviewed by the Green Ribbon Task Force for five hours as part of the investigation. They never once mentioned the murders. They focused on Bernardo being the

Scarborough Rapist, and his mistreatment of Karla. Yet it was hoped that Karla would be smart enough to make the connection, and realise the police suspected her husband of being the Green Ribbon killer, and if she had any information, she would tell them. Karla suddenly realised that if Paul broke first and told the police everything, then she was looking at spending the best part of the rest of her life in prison. So later that same evening she told her auntie and uncle that Paul was the Scarborough Rapist, and that he had killed Leslie Mahaffy and Kristen French.

When Karla had worked for the veterinary practice she had helped to treat a Dalmatian dog that was suffering from cancer, the dog belonged to a lawyer by the name of George Walker. Karla hired Walker and instructed him to try and arrange a plea bargain, in return for complete immunity from prosecution she would give the police Paul Bernardo's head on a platter. Walker approached Ray Houlahan of the St Catherine's Crown Criminal Law

Office, after some consideration, he refused a full immunity deal, after all, Houlahan didn't know the full extent of how involved Karla Bernardo had been in the murders and rapes. Then on Friday the 19th of February 1993, the police carried out a search of the Bernardo's home, they found that Paul Bernardo had egotistically kept detailed records of each of the rapes he had carried out. They also found one video containing footage of Paul Bernardo's "wedding present," the rape and sexual assault on the young girl that the Bernardo's had befriended and drugged some years before. The tape showed Karla enthusiastically performing acts of lesbianism on the unconscious underage girl. Importantly from the prosecutor's point of view, it proved that Karla had solid information they could use to prosecute her husband, and had committed crimes worthy enough to seek a plea deal herself. With this new evidence, George Walker entered into negotiations with Murray Segal, a plea bargaining expert from the Crown Criminal Law Office. After hours of negotiations a deal was brokered,

Karla would plead guilty to two acts of sexual assault, for which she would receive two twelve year sentences to run concurrently, the Crown Criminal Law Office would then liaise with the prison parole board, and ensure that Karla would be out of prison within three years. Karla Bernardo accepted the deal and was laughing all the way to her prison cell, and beyond to an expedient release date. It was a plea deal the pressed later dubbed "The Deal With The Devil." It caused public outrage when the true extent of Karla's actions in the murders became known, a deal the Crown Criminal Law Office began to deeply regret, but which they had no other option than to legally stand by.

Karla Bernardo's self-serving confessions as part of her plea deal began with a letter to her parents and sister, it read:

Dear Mom, Dad and Lori.

This is the hardest letter I've ever had to write, and you'll probably all hate me once you read it. I've kept this inside myself for so long, and I just can't lie to you anymore. Both Paul and I are responsible for Tammy's death. Paul was 'in love' with her and wanted to have sex with her. He wanted me to help him. He wanted me to get sleeping pills from work to drug her with. He threatened me and physically and emotionally abused me when I refused. No words I can say can make you understand what he put me through. So stupidly I agreed to do as he said. But something maybe the combination of drugs and the food she ate that night caused her to vomit. I tried so hard to save her. I am so sorry. But no words I can say can bring her back I would gladly give my life for hers. I don't expect you to ever forgive me, for I will never forgive myself.

Karla XXX

The next manoeuvre in her plea deal was a psychiatric assessment, which was biased in her favour, the produced document gave the following opinion, "Karla knew what was happening but felt utterly helpless, and unable to act in her own defence, or in anyone else's defence. She was, in my opinion, paralysed with fear and in that state became obedient and self-serving." Well, the psychiatrist certainly had one facet right.

One thing that puzzled the police and Karla was just what had happened to the sex tapes the couple had made featuring their victims? The answer was simple, Paul Bernardo had snatched them away at the first whiff of an arrest and had given them to his attorney for safekeeping. Ken Murray was under strict instructions not to give the tapes to the prosecution. So, for seventeen months he hoarded the vital evidence, which, it was later argued in court, directly contributed to Karla Bernardo receiving her plea deal. If the state had been given access to the tapes from the moment Murray was in possession of them, then Karla's testimony would not have been needed so badly, and Karla too may have been facing a murder charge and a life sentence. When Murray did decide to hand the tapes over to the prosecution team, he didn't do so in any straightforward manner. Murray approached the prosecution and asked for a plea deal for Paul Bernardo. Unbelievably Murray argued for Bernardo to be able to plead guilty to second-degree murder, with a minimum fifteen-year jail term, after this, he would be eligible for and looked at favourably for parole. What did the Crown get out of the deal? Well, they got to spare the families of Leslie Mahaffy and Kristen French from seeing footage of their beloved children being tortured and raped in their final hours. The tapes were, in Murray's words, "Humiliating to the memory of their (the families) children." The prosecution said the deal was a no-go, Bernardo would stand trial for first-degree murder and nothing else. Furthermore, they demanded the evidence Murray was withholding. After Bernardo's trial was over, Murray was arrested and charged with obstructing justice. In June of 2000, the Law Society of Upper Canada decided to progress no further with the charges against Murray. However, the damage to Murray's career was done. His reputation was irreparably damaged by trying to protect the interests of Canada's most reviled killer, Murray commented bitterly years later, "If you can't convict them, at least you can ruin them, but unfortunately that's what they did to me."

With Murray off the case and the tapes now in the hands of the prosecution team, it gave everyone a much clearer picture of just what they were dealing with, and just how up to her neck in it Karla Bernardo had been. Finally, it allowed Paul Bernardo to stand trial for two counts of first-degree murder, two counts of kidnapping, two counts of aggravated sexual assault, two counts of forcible confinement and one count of performing an indignity on a human body. When the trial opened on Thursday the 18th of May 1995, it did so in a shocking manner the likes of which no other trial had ever started in before. Crown Prosecutor Ray Houlahan pressed play on a video player, and footage appeared on-screen showing the crown's star witness masturbating herself into a frenzy. Houlahan told the court that this segment demonstrated how completely under Paul Bernard's will Karla had been, it highlighted the fact that she was willing to do anything to keep her man happy and in love with her. The trial itself was relatively straightforward. There was video evidence of Paul Bernardo committing the crimes, and the star witness testimony of his wife, who could attest to having witnessed him commit the atrocious crimes. Therefore no-one was at all surprised when on Friday the 1st of September 1995, after listening to the testimony of eighty-six witnesses and deliberating for eight hours, the jury returned a guilty verdict against Paul Bernardo. Bernardo was sentenced to life imprisonment with a minimum tariff of twenty-five years.

In the wake of the trial, and with both couples in prison, their murderous relationship truly broke down, and over the following years, they descended into bickering, mudslinging and bitter allegations. Each couple blamed the other for the whole sorry and sickening chain of events, and for escalating the cycle of rape, abuse and murder. Paul Bernardo was placed in virtual solitary confinement in one of Canada's scariest maximum security prisons, Kingston Penitentiary. He is locked in his cell for twenty-three hours a day for his own protection because so many other prisoners want to do him an extreme physical discourtesy. It hasn't stopped attempts to hurt him, though, Bernardo was assaulted 1996 as he was returned to his cell from the showers, and in 1999 a full-scale riot broke out in the prison when inmates tried to storm the segregation unit to get at

Bernardo. Paul Bernardo is aware that he probably will never be released from the Canadian penal system. He has been informed that he cannot apply for parole until at least 2020, and he has also been labelled by the courts as a Dangerous Offender. Under Canadian law, this means that Bernardo is one of only twenty-four criminals deemed too dangerous to be released back into society, and will in all probability remain in prison until the day he dies. Karla, on the other hand, spent most of her time in a relatively relaxed medium-security prison. Joliette Prison became more popularly known in the tabloid press as Club Fed, due to its easy-going and lacks routines. Here Karla was allowed to mingle freely with other prisoners and attend girly sorority like functions which included lemonade, cakes and other treats. She gave the tabloid press much to write about when it emerged that she had found herself a lesbian lover in prison and that she intended to live with her newfound beau upon release. Then as Karla grew nearer to her parole date, things began to go terribly wrong for her. She was photographed at one of the prison "parties" frolicking with a fellow inmate, who was serving time for aiding and abetting in a rape. Both were modelling skimpy cocktail dresses for their fellow inmates. The "Party Girl" photos caused an immediate backlash and public outcry. The prison authorities panicked and decided that Karla had to be moved to harsher surroundings, so she was shipped from the rather relaxed environs of Joliette Prison to the maximum-security Saskatoon Regional Psychiatric Facility. Karla was horrified and morally enraged. She took to protesting via none compliance with prison programs, and as a result, the prison authority had no other option than to gleefully defer her parole for four more years. The press and public were delighted. Her case for parole wasn't helped by an assessment that suggested Karla was simulating the psychological effects of spousal abuse, aided by reading about the symptoms in self-help books. A further psychological report read "(Karla) remains something of a diagnostic mystery. Despite her ability to present herself very well, there is a moral vacuity in her which is difficult, if not impossible, to explain." It wasn't the first time Karla would be turned down by the parole board, every couple of years she went before the board, and every couple of years she was flatly denied parole. By 2003 the various officials involved in making the decision decided that enough was enough, and they revoked Karla's right to apply for any further paroles until her sentence expiry date. In other words, Karla would serve the whole of her allotted twelve years imprisonment. Officially the two reasons given for this ruling were Karla's continued refusal to engage with psychiatric programs and her sexual relationship with a fellow inmate. This relationship indicated to the psychiatric experts that Karla still had sexually aggressive tendencies, which would make her an ongoing danger to the public. It was a bitter victory for the families of her victims who had argued for so long that Karla should serve her full twelve years.

The ruling created a slight problem if Karla were released on her sentenced expiry date it meant she would be released into the community unchecked. There would be no parole officers watching over her, monitoring her behaviour and looking for the telltale signs of risk that indicated she might still be a danger to the public. In June 2005 a special court session had to be convened at the Quebec Superior Court, where the state had to prove that Karla Bernardo posed an ongoing risk to the public. As such, they argued, she should be continually monitored by professionals after her sentence expiry date passed, and that her DNA should be kept on file so that it could be compared to DNA found at the scenes of any future murders or sex crimes that occurred after her release. Supreme Court Judge Jean Beaulieu agreed with the state, and she ruled that Karla Bernardo posed a continuing and ongoing risk to the public. After her release, Karla would have to inform the police of all her movements. Inform them where she intended to stay every night. Give the police seventy-eight hours notice if she planned to be away from home for more than forty-eight hours. She was not to contact Paul Bernardo. She was not to communicate with the relatives of her victims. She was not allowed contact with children under the age of sixteen, and she was to submit herself for regular psychiatric testing and therapy. Karla was reported to have been furious. This was in direct violation of her original plea bargain. She had been forced to serve nine years longer than the prosecutors promised her, and now she was going to be subjected to onerous restrictions, probably for the rest of her life. Her lawyers appealed the decision, calling the ruling "unconstitutional." They wanted every last requested restriction abandoned. In an attempt to boost her case Karla appeared on national television, from her prison cell, and told the nation how truly sorry, she was for the murders. The interview massively backfired. Karla came across as fake, facile, and above all, self-serving. Despite backing from some senators who felt that the conditions placed on Karla were "totalitarian," the appeal failed.

On Monday the 4th of July 2005, Karla Homolka (now calling herself Karla Teale) was released from St-Anne-des-Plaines prison. She gave an interview to a French-language radio station, where she stated that she had "paid her debt to society legally." In the years after her release, Karla was able to quickly move on with her life. Incredibly she married her lawyer's brother, Thierry Bordelais, and the pair moved to the Caribbean island of Guadeloupe. There, free from the restrictions placed on her by the Canadian government, Karla changed her name to Leanne Bordelais and now has a family of her own, two sons and a daughter. Perhaps this is fitting, for now, maybe the life sentence the world believed Karla Homolka deserved is truly starting, for every time Karla looks into her children's eyes, her daughters especially, she will remember her young victims, and the horrors that she and Paul Bernardo subjected them to.

The Last Supper: Katherine Knight and John Price

"She finds death attractive, the way some of us would view art." **- Dr Leah Giarratano on Katherine Knight**

Katherine Mary Knight had a history of mentally unstable and violent behaviour. From her very first relationship, she was the perpetrator of domestic violence and made every single one of her sexual partner's lives a misery. Her well-known reputation for vile behaviour should have been a warning to anyone who tried to get close to her. Unfortunately, one man did not heed the warning signs, he entered into a relationship with Knight, and it ended in a horror the likes of which is usually only seen in the most ludicrous of horror movie plots.

Katherine Mary Knight was born in Moree, New South Wales, Australia, on Monday the 24th of October 1955. Knight's birth had caused a major scandal in the nearby tiny town of Aberdeen. Knight's mother, Barbara Roughan, was married to the owner of the local abattoir, Jack Roughan. Jack was a powerful man in the town of Aberdeen as he happened to be the town's primary employer. Barbara played a dangerous game and had an affair with one of her husband's employees, Ken Knight. When Barbara fell pregnant with Ken Knight's offspring, the respective partners of the adulterous couple found out about the illicit relationship, and all hell broke loose. Both Barbara and Ken Knight were forced to leave town. Barbara had four sons, but Jack Roughan wouldn't let any of the children go with their mother. Instead, he kept the two oldest children and sent the two youngest to live with his sister in Sydney. It was into this miasma of heartbreak and dysfunction that Katherine Knight and her twin sister, Joy, were born. It was a busy household. Barbara and Ken Knight had a further two children after the birth of the twins, and in 1959 Jack Roughan passed away, and as a result, the two sons who lived with him from Barbara's relationship with Jack came to live with the Knight's. It was a desperately unhappy household. Ken Knight was a violent alcoholic with a high sex drive. He would get tanked up on a daily basis and demand sex from Barbara. If Barbara refused, he would simply rape her, sometimes in front of his young children. Discipline in the household was brutal, Ken Knight had a *"kilting stick"* which he kept in the hallway of the family home. He would liberally use this stick to chastise the children in the most demeaning of ways. He would use the stick to flog the children regularly until they were covered in painful, bleeding lacerations and bruises. On top of this psychical abuse, several family members sexually abused Katherine Knight and her siblings. In her adult life, Knight was studied by clinical psychologist Dr Leah Giarratano, she stated that this catalogue of traumas in her impressionable pre-school years was central to the violent personality she developed in later life and also are key to why Knight was able to commit such a horrific crime, "B*y the age of three or four something would already have died inside of* Katherine. *She knew no one was coming to make things better, she had to learn to fight or to hide. Obviously very young children can't fight back, so some will disassociate... Katherine was overwhelmed, and she mentally disconnected. Whilst she was in that state she was missing out on developing the range of emotions that make us human... love, happiness, joy and empathy.*"

Barbara Knight became a classic battered wife, her self-worth and self-confidence were destroyed by Ken Knight. Seeing the domestic disharmony in the Knight household coloured Katherine Knight's view of relationships. This warped view of sex and healthy relationships wasn't helped by the motherly advice that Barbara Knight gave to her daughter. When Katherine Knight's first boyfriend attempted to instigate intercourse, this frightened young Knight, she after all associated sex with violence and fear and abuse. She ran home to tell her mother about what had happened, Barbara Knight rather unhelpfully told her daughter that unwanted sexual advances were something she had to, *"Put up with and stop complaining."*

Knight and her twin sister attended Muswellbrook High School, here Knight began to act out the violent behaviours she had learnt throughout her childhood. She became a feared, violent, bully with few friends. She even bullied and beat her own twin sister. It was said that Knight particularly enjoyed picking on the very small children, dominating their lives completely and making their every hour of schooling utterly miserable. Dr Leah Giarratano was of the belief that even by this young juncture Katherine Knight was a hopeless case, *"She delighted in making people scared of her. Her destiny was set in stone at least by early adolescence, she was already really violent, and she was fantasising about violence, she was incapable of feeling true empathy, true love towards anybody.*" Even the teachers at Muswellbrook learnt to be scared of Knight after the young girl violently assaulted a teacher who'd attempted to chastise her for her unruly behaviour. Knight did have periods where she managed to settle down into her classes, and as an incentive, she would receive rewards for her good behaviour, but it never lasted. Knight left school at fifteen having learnt very little, she was completely illiterate, and her only prospects were finding low paid manual work or marrying someone who could provide for her. She initially became a cloth cutter at a local clothing factory, but in 1971 she got what she described as her "*dream job*" at the abattoir in Aberdeen. It was said that she took a "*malevolent pleasure*," in watching the animals die. Some even reported that when slaughtering the cows rather than slitting the cow's throat quickly and completely across for a quick death, she would only make a small incision into an artery and watch as the cows bled out slowly. Dr Leah Giarratano saw the abattoir has having fulfilled an important role in

Knight's life. It allowed her to sate her bloodlust, to enjoy the screams and squeals of the slaughtered animals and to *"get off"* on the fear the situation instilled in the doomed and dying animals, and to a degree her work colleagues. Nevertheless, Knight was seen as a good worker by the management, and she quickly moved up the various positions in the abattoir from offal cutter to boner, for which job the company supplied her with a set of knives. Knight was extremely proud of this achievement, and from that very day until the day she was locked up, the knives were hung proudly from the wall behind her bed. These knives were her *"most treasured possession,"* and she would fly into a rage if anyone dared to touch them. Knight's future husband would later say of these knives, *"She was totally and utterly possessed by knives. They were her life."*

In 1973, Katherine Knight met a young man who had come to work at the abattoir, he was called David Kellett but was affectionately known as "Shorty" due to his diminutive stature. Almost immediately, Knight entered into a tumultuous whirlwind romance with Kellett. Kellett was a heavy drinker with a temper. His temper usually led to him getting into barroom brawls, unusually Katherine Knight seemed to love this, and she revelled in the opportunity of Kellett starting a fight so that she could wade into the situation fists first. Less than a year after first meeting Knight and Kellett married. Both were very drunk from the moment they turned up at the registry office. Kellett's mother, Florence, was unsure about the match. Not that she was snobbish, but she felt that the Knight family were a little peculiar, *"There was always something about the family I wasn't sure of, I just felt there was a roughness around the edges,"* as Florence would later put it. On the wedding day, Barbara Knight gave her new son-in-law some motherly advice about his new wife, *"You better watch this one or she'll fucking kill you. Stir her up the wrong way or do the wrong thing and you're fucked, don't ever think of playing upon her, she'll fucking kill you. She's got something loose. She's got a screw loose somewhere."* Barbara Knight's words were only too prescient for less than twelve hours after exchanging vows Katherine Knight did indeed attempt to murder her husband. The couple had gone back to their marital home and got down to consummating the marriage. Despite being very intoxicated after just ending a two-day drinks binge, David Kellett managed to have sexual intercourse with Knight three times, before falling into a drunken stupor. This enraged Knight, she had envisioned her wedding night as a sex-fuelled orgy lasting from dusk to dawn. Her own parents had consummated their marriage five times on their wedding night, and Knight expected no less of her first night as a married woman. When she wasn't able to rouse her new husband from his drunken slumber, Knight climbed on top of Kellett placed her hands around his neck and began choking the life out of him. Luckily for Kellett, Knight failed in her attempt to murder her husband, but from that moment on, she made David Kellett's life a misery. Knight was prone to violent outbursts at the slightest provocation, *"She would snap like a biscuit,"* David Kellett would say in interview years later, *"It wouldn't take much to set her off, the slightest thing."* She would verbally and physically berate and bully Kellett, physical violence became a daily norm, followed by short periods where Knight was the most loving person in the world. Kellett got some respite from his predicament when his sister came to live with the couple for a few short months. When Sandy Kellett arrived, David Kellett gave his sister a word of warning, *"If she gets cranky just get out of the way because if she picks up a knife, it's too late."* Despite these words of warning, Knight seemed to become charm itself for a few short weeks, and Sandy began to wonder what her brother had been talking about. Sandy Kellett later admitted that she was completely fooled by Knight, and they became firm friends. It was all an act, of course. Perpetrators of domestic violence are magnificent at manipulation and playing the charmer when it suits, and Katherine Knight was no different. Eventually, the mask slipped when one day Knight entered into one of her rages. Sandy Kellet retold the story years later, *"She was extremely happy... and the next minute she just flew into a rage... she got this strength about her, she became so strong that she could have picked David up and thrown him across the room."* The experience of seeing an unwarranted violent outburst first-hand frightened Sandy Kellett, and soon after she packed her bags and left.

The violence all came to a head just under two years after Kellett and Knight had exchanged vows. By this period Knight was heavily pregnant with her first child, Melissa. David Kellett returned home late one night from a darts match to discover that Knight had burnt all his clothes. As he stood in despair wondering what he had done to deserve such a dog's life, Knight snuck up behind him and cracked him over the back of the head with an iron, severely fracturing his skull. Knight attempted to strike Kellett with the iron a second time, but he managed to stagger to the safety of a neighbour's house. Kellett was rushed to the hospital and was treated for the skull fracture, he spent two days in a coma before recovering consciousness. As he spent the next few weeks in the hospital, Kellett realised that enough was enough, and he decided to leave Knight and move as far away as he possibly could from his murderous wife. He went to live in Queensland, leaving Knight to bring up Melissa by herself.

After the birth of baby Melissa in May 1976, Knight began to suffer from post-natal depression. This manifested itself in Knight attempting to harm her baby daughter. Neighbours became concerned one day when they saw Knight shake baby Melissa and act as if she was about to push her pram into oncoming traffic. The police were called, and Knight was interviewed. The police realised that Knight was clearly mentally very unwell, and she was taken to St Elmo's Hospital in nearby Tamworth for treatment. When Knight's mood stabilised thanks to some anti-depressants, she was released from St Elmo's, and baby Melissa was put straight back into Knight's care. Knight responded to her parental duties by immediately making an attempt on her baby daughter's life. She put Melissa in her pram and left the pram on a set of rail tracks. Knight then headed into Aberdeen where she picked up an axe which had been left abandoned in a garden, and she proceeded to walk through the town waving the axe around her head shouting threats and generally menacing the populace. As Knight was making a nuisance of herself in the town centre, baby Melissa was rescued from a near-fatal train collision. A local shop owner called Lorna Driscol had watched from a distance as Knight put baby Melissa onto the train tracks. Ms Driscol shouted for help, and a local hobo named "Old Ted" Abrahams placed his life in his hands by stepping in front of the oncoming coal train and pulling the child to safety with just seconds to spare. Once again, Knight was arrested and taken to St Elmo's Hospital to be psychiatrically assessed.

Despite clear warning signs that Knight was deeply mentally unwell, she discharged herself just a few short hours after her admittance. The next day Knight persuaded her neighbour that baby Melissa was unwell and needed to be taken to the nearest hospital. The neighbour agreed readily to help the sick child. Knight disappeared into her house, the neighbour followed, only to find Kathrine's mood had turned on a dime and that she was in one of her explosive rages. Knight produced a knife and began chasing the neighbour and their teenage daughter around the house and into the front garden. The teenager got into a tussle with Knight, and the young girl found her face being slashed by the blade. The family were petrified, and Knight proceeded to hold them hostage at knifepoint. Knight's thinking was confused and irrational. She began saying that she wanted to go to Florence Kellett's house and murder her mother-in-law in revenge for her husband having abandoned her. Then Knight demanded that they drive to Queensland, where she was going to take her revenge out directly on David

Kellett.   The petrified neighbour and her bleeding daughter sat in their car as Knight menacingly pointed the bloodied blade of the knife at them. Before leaving the town to make the 1300 mile journey to Queensland, Knight demanded that the neighbour pull over into a local service station. Filled with fear for both herself and her bloodstained and injured daughter, the neighbour agreed.   As soon as she'd pulled the car to a halt an unspoken understanding passed between mother and daughter and the two women jumped from the car as one and ran into the garage for help. The mechanics in the garage saw Katherine Knight storming towards them, pausing briefly to further arm herself with a metal rod. The mechanics used these vital seconds to lock themselves safely indoors. Knight was enraged. She responded by grabbing hold of a small boy as he ran towards his parents and holding the knife to his throat she demanded that the garage owner come out and face her. The police arrived, Knight continued to hold the knife to the boy's throat and waved the metal rod menacingly at the police. Somehow one of the officers was able to disarm Knight by knocking the weapons from her hands using nothing more than a broomstick. Knight was immediately taken to Morisset Psychiatric Hospital, where another psychiatric assessment was undertaken. Knight informed the doctors that she had intended to kill the garage owner as he had recently completed work on David Kellett's car, making it roadworthy enough for him to flee his marriage. After killing the garage owner Knight had intended to drive to Florence Kellett's home to murder her mother-in-law, before finally moving onto Queensland where she would have killed her estranged husband.

Now this time, the doctors were not willing to release Knight unless someone took responsibility for her care. Knight's own family wanted nothing to do with her. So, unbelievably it was Florence Kellett who stepped up to the plate and agreed to take responsibility for Knight. When David Kellett heard about what had happened, rather than being ever more fearful for his life, he made the decision to return to Aberdeen and help his mother care for his estranged wife. In a way, David Kellett felt responsible for Knight's condition. Living with Kellett under his mother's roof seemed to soothe Knight's mood, and for a time, David Kellett remembered why he had fallen in love with Knight in the first place. Soon after being released Knight, David, Florence and baby Melissa moved to Woodridge in Brisbane. All parties felt that an entirely fresh start would help in Katherine's rehabilitation. Before they left, however, there was one last violent incident. The Kellett family stopped off at the Knight household so that Knight could say goodbye to her parents. Barbara Knight strode determinedly out of the house, leant into the car and began to strangle David Kellett. Barbara Knight's grip on David Kellett's throat was so great he couldn't prise her fingers from around his neck. His face was going red, his eyes were bulging, and he began to pass out. Florence Kellett and Katherine Knight were under no illusions that Barbara

Knight was determined to murder David Kellett. Knight responded by jumping out of the car, running over to her mother and raining blow after blow down upon her mother's head. One punch landed squarely on the back of Barbara Knight's head and knocked her down to the floor, unconscious. David Kellett sat at the wheel of the car gasping for breath as Knight calmly climbed back in alongside him and chirpily told David to drive on.

In Woodridge Knight recovered mentally, and eventually felt well enough to take up work at Dinmore meatworks. For four years Kellett and Knight continued to play happy families if occasionally punctuated by bouts of domestic violence. It seems though that perhaps Knight had begun to take her anger out on her children. It is from Sandy Kellett that we have evidence of this, an event that years later still brought tears to Sandy's eyes. One evening when Sandy had come to visit her brother she heard Mellissa Knight screaming in agony in the bathroom. Sandy went running in to see what was happening, only to find Katherine Knight holding baby Mellissa in the bathtub under a scalding hot water tap. Sandy Kellett didn't hesitate in going straight to her brother to tell him of the abuse she had just seen Knight inflict upon the young child. David Kellett suddenly became very fearful and begged his sister not to saying anything as Knight would, *"Kill you in your sleep, and most likely then kill me."*

In 1979 Knight fell pregnant again, Natasha Maree was born on Thursday the 6th of March 1980. Despite her earlier histrionic antics when David Kellett left her, it was Knight who was now becoming bored of the marriage. Arguments had increased between the pair, and bitter acrimony had fallen over the marriage. David Kellett was still petrified of Knight and was actually somewhat glad when he discovered that she was now having an affair with another man. Now she was not obsessing about Kellett, Knight's jealousy seemed to abate slightly. Kellett had also gotten a job as a long-distance lorry driver, a job which mercifully for him took him all over the country for long periods. In early 1984 Knight decided that the marriage was well and truly dead. One day when Kellett was off on one of his long haul jobs, Knight packed up all of her belongings, took the children and moved back to Aberdeen to live with her parents. Kellett returned to find the family home empty and abandoned.

By 1986 Knight was out of work after an injury to her back and living in social housing in Aberdeen with Melissa and Natasha Maree. This was when a thirty-eight-year-old former speedway driver and miner by the name of David Saunders came on the scene. Again this relationship was marred by heavy drinking and violence. Knight was insanely suspicious of Saunders. Despite the fact he spent most of the time living with Knight; Saunders refused to give up an apartment he owned in the nearby town of Scone, and Knight believed it was because Saunders was having all sorts of affairs. In May 1987 Knight contrived the perfect way of illustrating to Saunders what consequences he would face if Knight ever did find out he was having an affair. Knight got Saunders' pet dingo puppy and slit its throat as Saunders helplessly watched on agog. When Saunders angrily attempted to remonstrate with Knight, she simply smashed him over the head with a frying pan, knocking him unconscious. This episode was an indication of Katherine Knight's true psychopathic nature. She showed a deep lack of empathy for the suffering of the helpless creature she so callously killed but displayed an understanding of how the death would affect the emotions of her partner. Perhaps we shouldn't be surprised that Knight was so coldly willing to murder a defenceless animal simply to prove a point. Research from the University of Denver shows us that 60% of those who have been abused or witnessed domestic violence go on to abuse family pets or other animals. Now, if my girlfriend slit the throat of my puppy dog, I would cut and run and thank my lucky stars that it wasn't my throat she'd slit. Not David Saunders, oh no, he hung around. Why? Well, the answer was quite simple and rather childish, both Kellett and Saunders said that they stayed around for much longer than they should have done because the sex with Knight was "*fantastic.*" As one of Knight's friends would later comment, "*She was mad with sex, she'd do it anywhere, anytime, anyhow, and with anyone.*"

In late 1987 Saunders impregnated Knight, and in June 1988 Knight gave birth to another baby daughter, who she called Sarah. Saunders finally sold his apartment in Scone and bought a house with Knight, ready to settle down and be a family man. Finally living together permanently, with no place to escape the arguments and jealous rages, the domestic violence grew in the relationship. Some of the violence became quite psychological, such as Knight turning up at a family members houses armed with a shotgun and telling the family member that she had murdered Saunders. Dr Leah Giarratano believes that Knight did such things for two reasons, firstly, because she enjoyed seeing people upset and distressed, and secondly, it was all part of Knight preparing psychologically for a real murder. Knight had a fantasy in her mind of murdering Saunders, the one thing missing from the fantasy was experiencing his friends and family's upset when they found out about Saunders death. So, by telling his friends and family that she had murdered Saunders', and watching their shock, horror and distress, it made her fantasy all the more real and therefore, all the more enjoyable.

Just a few short weeks after moving in together Knight made another murderous attempt on David Saunders life. She hit Saunders in the face with an iron, dazing and confusing him, and as he staggered around trying to get his bearings, Knight stabbed him the stomach with a pair of scissors. Like David Kellett before him, Saunders was able to make it to the safety of a neighbour's house, where the neighbour called an ambulance. Saunders was so scared he went into hiding for several months. Eventually, he plucked up the courage to return to his former family home to see his daughter. He found the house abandoned, his clothes left behind cut up and burnt. Soon after Saunders found himself being arrested by the police and being issued with an Apprehended Violence Order[v]. It seems that despite her being the instigator of the domestic violence Knight had gone to the police to tell them that she was in fear of Saunders and his explosive temper. Whatever way you look at this outcome, Saunders had a very lucky escape.

Knight next shacked herself up with a forty-three-year-old abattoir worker named John Chillingworth. The relationship was just as abusive as all the others, it involved lots of heavy drinking and lots of explosive arguments and lots of jealousy. Knight quickly fell pregnant and gave birth to a son who she called Eric.

Despite her own volcanic jealousy, which was the cause of most of the domestic disharmony, it was Knight who had an affair. The affair was with a thirty-eight-year-old local miner called John Price, known as Pricey to his friends. He was a man who seemed to be universally loved, and who no one had a bad word to say about, as one local put it, *"He was a terrific bloke who'd give you his left arm if you needed it."* Pretty soon Knight was head over heels in love with Price, and in 1995 Knight kicked Chillingworth out of the family home so that she could enter into a full-blown relationship with Price. Price like most of Knight's previous lovers liked a drink. Indeed, researcher, Peter Lalor concluded that *"There was rarely a night in their lives when they were sober, especially when they were with Knight."*

Price was a divorcee who lived with two of his three children. After initially liking Knight, Price's eldest daughter, Rose, learnt to fear and then hate Knight. It started with stories from her younger sister, Rebecca.

One day early on in the relationship Knight had been driving Rebecca to school when Knight deliberately veered the car across to the other side of the road so that she could intentionally run over a dog. Rebecca was stunned and distressed by this bizarrely cruel act, she asked Knight why she'd done it, and Knight simply replied, *"I don't like dogs."* Then on another occasion, Knight sat Rebecca Price down and told her that John Price wasn't her real father. Knight told Rebecca that her mother had been unfaithful to her father and that Rebecca had been the unwanted result of that illicit affair. This conversation reduced Rebecca to inconsolable tears, but highly amused Knight who thought it was the funniest joke ever. Then Rose heard the rumours around the town about Knight's violent behaviour in previous relationships. The tales of her murdering puppy dogs and stabbing her lovers. Rose grew to believe that Knight was a psychopath who would ultimately end up hurting her father. She begged her father on several occasion to end his relationship with Katherine Knight, but Price refused. You see, to begin with, the couple were in the honeymoon stage, where Knight was on her best behaviour and wasn't subject to her volcanic explosions of jealous rage, and charmed Price with her sexual talents.

It wasn't long before the old behaviours set in. Jealousy crept back into Knight's heart. Knight began to badger Price to marry her. Price kept refusing. The more he refused, the angrier and angrier Knight became. In revenge Knight took the family video recorder and filmed inside of Price's garage. The camera lingered on a $20 medical kit which was quite clearly labelled property of the Mining Company which Price worked for. Knight then sent this video to Price's boss. Now, Price might have had many faults, he might have been more than a little rough and ready, but he was actually as honest as the day was long. Price explained that the medical kit had been out of date and had been thrown out by the company's Health and Safety Officer, he'd recovered it from the bins so he could use it if he or his children had an accident at home. His explanation did no good, rules were rules, and even taking a piece of apparatus destined for the scrap heap was seen in the eyes of the company as theft by an employee. The management dismissed Price from the well-paid position he'd held for seventeen years and told him that he was lucky not to be facing prosecution for the theft. Price returned home and immediately threw Knight out on her ears. Knight begged forgiveness, but Price was determined that that was the end of the relationship. Knight also discovered that the townsfolk had turned their backs on her too. Price was well-loved in the local community, and you didn't just destroy a man's livelihood because you'd had a domestic disagreement.

It seems that Knight had a silken tongue, for despite having ruined his career and livelihood, within weeks of the incident, Knight wormed her way back into Price's bed. Knight told her daughter Natasha that the only way

Price was now going to get out of the relationship was if he were dead. Rose Price was beside herself with worry. She wondered how her father could be so stupid. Rose pleaded with Price to end the relationship. Her pleas became ever more insistent and desperate as the relationship became more and more violent. During 1999 Knight had attacked Price on three separate occasions with a bladed article and had a caused him injuries which required hospital treatment. At first, Price kept trying to end the relationship, but Knight stubbornly refused to leave Price's family home. Things became worse when Knight discovered that she had not been included in Price's Last Will and Testament. Price had left all his worldly goods and assets to his ex-wife and children. Knight was incandescent with rage. She told Price that if he wanted to be rid of her, he would have to pay a price, a financial one, she wanted $10,000 as severance pay for wasting her last few good years of looks and fertility on the relationship. Price refused. He was by now living in abject fear of Knight but refusing to leave her. The reason he wouldn't end the relationship was that he feared for his children. Knight had made it clear that if he ended the relationship, then she would kill Price's offspring. Price now realised just how truly psychotic Knight was and that his life and possibly the lives of his children were in real danger.

One day in late 1999 Price reached out to Katherine Knight's former husband, David Kellett, for advice. They secretly met in a bar, and Price explained to Kellett that the violence was becoming too much for him. Kellett later said that Price was obviously in real fear, shaking profusely, he talked anxiously about Knight. What advice could Kellett give to Price about how to escape from Knight's clutches? How had he managed to get out of the relationship with his life? Kellett told Price that he had escaped through luck more than good judgement, and that Price should get out of the relationship as soon as he could, or the chances were Knight really would murder him. Kellett explained that

Price could get a restraining order against Knight, something Kellett never had the luxury of doing back in the 1970s and 80s when he was plagued by the Knight's horrific violent outbursts. Price left the meeting saying he would give the suggestion serious consideration.

On Tuesday the 29th of February 2000, there was one final violent row between Knight and Price. This time Knight attacked Price with a knife, and he was forced to flee his home and hide at a neighbours. The next day Price took David Kellett's advice. He went to the Scone Magistrates Court and attempted to get an injunction against Knight so she could not contact him or come near his home. It was here that Price suddenly found out that something unbelievable had happened. Knight had contacted the police before him, told them that Price was the instigator of the domestic violence and that she was in fear of Price. As a result, an Apprehended Violence Order had been put in place against Price. Price was now seen as the aggressor and Knight as the victim. Price was insistent that he wanted something done to protect him and his family from his girlfriend. The magistrate told Price that if he wanted to take out a Restraining Order, it would take the Court three weeks to fully assess the matter and put the order in place. Price was sent away with strict instructions to stay away from Katherine Knight, or he would be the one to face arrest. The first thing Price did as he dejectedly left the Courthouse was to telephone his boss at work and tell him that if he didn't come into work the next day, then his boss should contact the police because it would mean Katherine Knight had murdered him. Unbelievably Price was right.

Katherine Knight was stinging with anger at the thought of Price trying to assert control over his life again, so spitefully she carefully plotted Price's demise. Price sent his children to stay with some friends for the evening, he'd already confided in his co-workers that he was scared Knight was psychotic enough to murder his children. Then Price went to a neighbours to have a few drinks and hopefully avoid Knight if she did come calling. Price returned home and went to bed at about 11.00 p.m. At midnight Knight arrived. She silently let herself into the property as Price slept, showered, and slipped into some sexy negligée she had bought especially for the occasion. She went into Price's room, woke him and despite his earlier intention to throw Knight out on her ear, they ended up having sex. After copulation, Price fell asleep, and as he lay peaceful and defenceless Knight plunged a butcher's knife into his chest. Price immediately woke up screaming, he jumped up and tried to run down the hallway towards the front door, but Knight was right behind him, plunging the knife into his back as he attempted to escape. Price reached the front door, threw it open and staggered out into the street, only for Knight to grab Price from behind and drag him back into the house. Price fell to the floor, and Knight loomed over him and rained down a succession of blows with the knife. All in all, Knight stabbed Price thirty-seven times in an absolute frenzy. When the initial white anger of the frenzied attack had dissipated Knight coldly, calculatedly and carefully skinned Price's body using her abattoir knives. Price even removed notoriously difficult areas of the flesh such as Price's ears, scalp and fingertips and the flesh around his neck. Knight then hung the bloody skin from the architrave above the sitting-room door. Knight had been so careful and precise when skinning Price the pathologist, Dr Timothy Lyons, was later able to put the skin back onto the corpse after the autopsy. After skinning Price; Knight then set about cutting up the body and cooking it. She intended to serve up the roasted human meat to Price's children with accompanying seasonal vegetables and lashings of gravy. She'd laid the dinner table and put out placeholders indicating where each child should sit as they ate their father. Next to each placeholder was a photograph of the intended child which Knight had furiously and impudently stabbed several times with a knife. When the meat looked ready, she served some to the family dog and ate some herself. The meat Knight had placed in the oven to roast was from Price's buttocks, and it was too tough to chew and not very tasty, so Knight threw out the remainder of her plate onto the back lawn. Instead of serving the children roasted rump steak, Knight placed Price's decapitated head into a pot with boiling water and some vegetables in an attempt to make a stew. As the head stewed slowly on the cooker, Knight nipped out with Price's bankcard and took $1000 from an ATM machine[vi]. This money was never recovered, and one of the minor mysteries of the whole affair is just what Knight did with the $1000. Knight then returned to Price's house and rearranged his mutilated corpse, crossing the legs at the ankles, and placing his left arm over an empty bottle of Shelley's Club Lemon Squash. Dr Leah Giarratano was of the opinion that Knight, *"Took a lot of pride* (in the murder), *she saw this as her triumph… it takes an extreme amount of pressure or stress to get a psychopath to feel, and she would have been really revelling in that moment."* After taking some time to survey her handiwork, Knight wrote a suicide note which read, *"Time got you back Johnathon for rapping my douter. You to Beck for Ross – for Little John. Now play with little Johns dick John Price[vii]."* After writing the slanderous note, Knight took an ineffectual overdose of prescription pills and lay down on the bed where the murderous attack had begun just a few hours before. Knight fell into a deep slumber, but the suicide attempt would ultimately fail.

At 6.00 a.m. the next morning, Price's co-workers became concerned when Price did not arrive for work like he had prophesied. His boss decided to go and personally see if Price was okay. When he arrived at Price's house, he was chilled to find bloodstains on the front door. Immediately sensing that something was deeply amiss, he telephoned for the police. Sergeant Graham Furlong and Sergeant Scott Matthews were dispatched. Sergeant Matthews knew Price personally, and was a little worried, as he knew him as a hard and dependable worker, and this behaviour was deeply out of character. Furlong and Matthews arrived at the scene at 8.00 a.m. Receiving no answer when they knocked on the front door, they decided to enter the property via the back door. The two unsuspecting coppers entered the house of horrors little expecting what they would uncover or how it would affect their lives. They immediately found their line of sight blocked by what they took to be a curtain. Sergeant Matthews moved the curtain aside with his left hand, and both officers could immediately see the skinned and headless body of John Price lying in the hallway. Sergeant Matthews suddenly realised that the curtain he had just so casually pushed aside had been the flayed skin of the victim, he looked down, and his arm was covered in blood. Both the officers were shocked and sickened by the sight of the mutilated corpse. Both men immediately felt physically sick at being confronted with such an unexpected, haunting and macabre sight. Both officers immediately wanted to get away from the galling scene, so they moved on into the kitchen. Here there was a strange smell filling the small room, it emanated from the cooker, Sergeant Furlong immediately noticed the pot bubbling on the stove. Sergeant Furlong turned to Sergeant Matthews and muttered grimly, *"I'll give you one guess where the head is."* Matthews moved over to the pot and lifted the lid. What he saw boiling in the depths of the water made him gag and step back in horror. Sergeant Matthews threw the lid back down onto the pot and staggered away clutching at his mouth. After seeing such a keenly disturbing sight, Sergeant Matthews stated that Sergeant Furlong tried to comfort him, telling him it was going to be okay, and that they had to continue searching the house. Sergeant Furlong, however, was struggling to cope with the horrid sights around him, *"You get auditory exclusion... it was quite a frightening experience,"* he would comment years later. Despite quite clearly entering into shock, Sergeant Furlong knew he couldn't back out and leave his partner to search the rest of the house alone, *"Once you're in that situation there is just no backing out.*" As they walked down the main hallway, Furlong and Matthews could hear snoring loudly emanating from one of the bedrooms. Sergeant Matthews didn't mind admitting that he was filled with fear and by now had drawn his gun. They entered the room to find Katherine Knight, lying on the bed, fully clothed, snoring like a baby next to an empty packet of prescription painkillers. Sergeant Furlong immediately radioed for an ambulance. The officers tried to wake Knight, they semi-roused her, and then half carried half walked her to the rear of the property where they lay her down on the back lawn. It wasn't long before Katherine Knight was being rushed to the hospital to have her stomach pumped.

The sights the police uncovered in John Price's home deeply affected many of the investigating officers and those involved in the prosecution of the case. Scott Matthews told a reporter in 2014 that he had, "*endured years of therapy to try to wipe the vision* (of the house) *from my head.*" The presiding judge at the resultant trial Mr Justice Barry O'Keefe QC said, "*I can tell you I found this a very stressful matter, in fact, after it was over I didn't eat meat for about three months. The thought of meat reminded me of events in that house.*" That was after only having seen the scene of crime photographs and watching the video the police had made of the house. One of the most deeply affected was the man who headed the investigation, Detective Sergeant Bob Mills. Some years after the event, he admitted that the sights in Price's house caused him to suffer from Post-Traumatic Stress Disorder and have "*a nervous breakdown.*" He described quite emotionally how the terrifying abattoir-like scene devastated him and his colleagues, "*Walking into that crime scene it was horrific, carnage throughout the house, from one end to the other... Anyone who went into that house had a feeling of numbness for quite sometime afterwards before they came to actually registering what had actually happened... You just sort of lose the majority of your senses for a short period of time until you regather them, and realise that it was reality and not a horror scene... It's something I'm still trying to get to grips with even today, emotionally and mentally... How can any human do that to any other human?"*

Katherine Knight's trial began on Monday the 15th of October 2001 at the Newcastle Courthouse before Mr Justice Barry O'Keefe QC. Knight's lawyers immediately offered a plea deal, if the prosecution were willing to accept a plea of Manslaughter due to Knight suffering from diminished responsibility then she would be willing to plead guilty and avert the trial. Knight was claiming that she had absolutely no memory of the murder. She was willing to admit that she must have done it, but she wasn't responsible for her actions due to the years of abuse Price had put her through. Price must have turned violent again, and Knight must have just snapped, committing the murder like an automaton, and as such, she had no memory of doing such a terrible thing. If the prosecution accepted this as fact, then it would, of course, have attracted a much lighter sentence than if Knight were found guilty of coldblooded murder. The prosecution refused this proffered deal, for they had the sworn statement of Kathrine Knight's very own brother. Barry Knight told the police that his sister had admitted to him just three weeks before the murder that she was going to kill Price and do it in such a way that she would, *"get away with it… I'm going to do it in a way to make them think that I am crazy."* With the prosecution refusing the plea deal Knight defiantly pleaded Not Guilty to the charge of murder. The trial commenced with the prosecution showing the jury the video the police had made of the crime scene, Peter Lalor said of this, *"It is, perhaps, the most horrific video you would ever wish to see. It's just unimaginable what the police saw that day, and what was recorded on that video."* When the jury saw the true horror of what Katherine Knight had done, it made it so much harder for them to believe that the unassuming woman sat in the dock could have absolutely no memory of committing such a nightmarish and horrific act. An event which was no quick act of self-defence, but was rather undoubtedly cold and calculated and planned, and would have taken several hours to perpetrate. The crime scene video also played a part in Katherine Knight's trial and sentencing going largely unreported and unpublished in the media, as Peter Lalor explained, *"We had to make a decision whether the story was palatable for people to read with their breakfast in the morning. A decision was made this couldn't be reported. It was too horrific."*

On the second day of the trial Knight stunned everyone by changing her plea to Guilty, Mr Justice O'Keefe was worried that given her history of mental illness Knight didn't understand the seriousness of changing her plea at such a late stage. Mr Justice O'Keefe was concerned that as a result of the change of plea Knight would later use the judge's acceptance of the plea change as grounds for an appeal, and therefore get off the murder charge on a legal technicality. So, before he accepted the guilty plea, Mr Justice O'Keefe had Knight assessed by two psychiatrists, Dr Robert Delaforce and Dr Rod Milton. Dr Delaforce and Dr Milton both came to the same conclusion, Knight was suffering from a Borderline Personality Disorder, but was mentally sound enough to reason and understand the implications of her guilty plea. Dr Delaforce concluded his report with the damning statement, *"What she did on the night was part of her personality, her nature, herself, but it is not a feature of Borderline Personality Disorder. It is not even slightly connected."* Dr Milton also commented on Knight's wider mental state at the time of the murder, *"The problem is not that she did not know it was wrong to do such things but that she did not care... She had the ability to control herself at the time she killed. She could have decided not to kill him. I do not believe her ability to control herself was impaired... I think she obtained some satisfaction from the act. I realise this is not a very charitable thing to say, but there is a good reason to think there was some satisfaction or enjoyment in carrying out these kinds of acts."*

Mr Justice O'Keefe considered the expert opinion of the two psychiatrists and therefore accepted the change of plea and proceeded to sentence. Mr Justice O'Keefe was damning in his summation, *"The last minutes of his* (John Price) *life must have been a time of abject terror for him as they were a time of utter enjoyment for her... She has not expressed any contrition or remorse, and if released, she poses a serious threat to the security of society."* Katherine Knight became the first woman in Australian legal history to be sentenced to a whole life tariff, she will never be released from prison.

Katherine Knight's case should act as a stark warning to all those women and men in domestically abusive relationships as to what horrors may come. For it truly was a classic case of domestic abuse coming to its naturally brutal conclusion. As Dr Leah Giarratano explained, "*It wasn't about losing* (Price), *or losing his love, because Knight couldn't feel love. It was a lot more about control and owning the victim than it is about loss. So, when* (Knight) *wanted to, she moved on from her partners, but if they tried to move on from her, that's when she would exact her revenge.*"

The Unhappy Happy Ending: Helen Bailey and Ian Stewart

"Real life after death is far more bizarre, more complicated and quite frankly bonkers than any fiction plot that I could come up with." - Helen Bailey

Helen Bailey lived a charmed life, an author whose works of young adult fiction had made her a multi-millionaire. Her Electra Brown novels had seen her become *"Queen of Teen,"* fiction. Before becoming a writer, Helen had attended Thames Polytechnic, where she toyed with the idea of becoming a Forensic Scientist. In 1988 Helen got a job working as a temp for John Sinfield, the man who would become the great love of her life. Sinfield negotiated licences to market children's cartoon characters in the United Kingdom. He would buy the UK rights to cartoons like Rugrats or

Snoopy then licence the characters to people who wanted to make toys or put the cartoon's images on mugs, plates and lunchboxes. Helen's warmth made her good at buttering-up clients, and Sinfield realised that Helen would be a great asset to the Sinfield team. Given a permanent position Helen began to work in close collaboration with John Sinfield, and quite quickly the couple fell in love. After several years of courtship, they married in 1996 and spent the next fifteen years being utterly devoted to one another. It was John Sinfield who encouraged Helen to pursue a career as a writer, and in 2008 Helen's first wildly popular Electra Brown novel was published, quickly followed by a sequel later that very same year.

Helen's life was turned upside down on Sunday the 27th of February 2011, it was a nexus point in her life, a day that led not only to her husband's death but ultimately her own demise five years later. Holidaying in Barbados, John Sinfield went for a swim in the warm Caribbean waters, he was caught in a riptide and drowned. The event was shocking, unexpected and brutally fast, Helen Bailey put it so well herself; she had been "*a wife at breakfast, but a widow at lunch.*"

After her husband's death forty-six-year-old Helen was left in a world of grief, she was little equipped to deal with. Looking around for help and support, she found only indifference and loneliness. So, she used her skills as a writer to help herself and others. She began a blog called "Planet Grief" where she detailed her life as a widow and the tsunami of emotions her husband's death had caused. She detailed her life of loneliness and self-reflection, having to do things alone that she once did as a couple, her first Christmas without John, her having to go to places she would once go with her husband, and the pain this caused. Yet, she constantly was able to lace every post with moments of poignant stinging humour. Helen also began to reach out to other bereavement sites. One such community was on Facebook. Here she met the *"Gorgeous Grey Haired Widow"* who would seduce her, marry her and kill her for her fortune.

Ian Stewart was a fifty-one-year-old widow whose forty-seven-year-old wife, Diane, had died of a suspected epileptic seizure on Friday the 25th of June 2010[VIII]. Diane Stewart's death had been unexpected, she'd not suffered a seizure since her teenage years, her condition was controlled by medication, and she had been quite health-conscious, jogging and regularly going to the gym to do aerobics and other assorted classes. The doctors were baffled by her sudden death, so baffled, in fact, that two autopsies were carried out, and the authorities refused to issue either a death certificate or give Diane's body back to her family for six whole weeks. Due to the dubious and sudden nature of the seemingly healthy middle-aged woman's demise an inquest was held, the coroner found that Diane died of *"sudden unexpected death in epilepsy."* In the wake of Diane's death Ian Stewart raked in the cash, he received £16,000 from a

Legal and General policy, a £28,000 death in service severance payment from Cambridge County Council, and £33,000 from a life insurance policy. Stewart bought an MG sports car with the money he recouped from his wife's death, and began to wine and dine several young ladies. Soon after Diane's death, Stewart began to visit websites for widowers. Places were grieving people could exchange stories and receive support from others who had been through similar experiences. It was while on one of these sites that Ian Stewart first started corresponding with Helen Bailey.

The relationship between Helen and Ian Stewart was a whirlwind romance later described in court as *"love bombing."* Helen described Stewart in the dedication of her first book for adults, "When Bad Things Happen In Good Bikinis" as her *"Happy Ending."* They first met in October 2011. After chatting on a Facebook messaging board for some little time, Ian Stewart tracked Helen down. He turned up one evening unannounced and unbidden on her doorstep in Highgate, London. At first, Helen felt guilty about her growing feelings for Stewart, and she attempted to push him away on several occasions, but Stewart persisted. Stewart's determined advances left Helen feeling, "*sleazy, guilty and ashamed*," because she was beginning to feel happiness and feelings of attraction just eight short months after her beloved husband's death. Stewart persuaded Helen to go on a date, they went to see the big-screen adaptation of John le Carré's *Tinker, Tailor, Soldier, Spy*. Once again, after the date, Helen told Ian Stewart that it was too soon after her husband's death for her to be moving on. Yet again, Ian Stewart persisted, he persuaded Helen that they could take it slow, start off just going on walks with Helen's dachshund. On these bittersweet romantic walks love blossomed. It was when walking through Marks and Spencer's one day that Helen realised she was considering buying some sexy undies to wear on a date with Stewart and that she was falling for him. It's hard to actually see what Helen saw in the former software engineer. He was a little taller than Helen, overweight, unkempt, unshaven, with prominent uneven teeth and receding silver hair. Add to this tired eyes underlined by heavy bags which emphasised his demeanour as a man who was in need of a good rest. There was something of the faded Lothario about Ian Stewart. He had the look of a man past his prime, but who had found himself in a situation which made him as happy as a pig in swill.

In 2012 the couple moved into a £1.5 million mansion house complete with swimming pool, situated in the village of Royston in the heart of rural Hertfordshire. They called their mansion Hartwell Lodge, and Stewart's two adult sons, Jamie and Oliver, moved into the spacious property with the couple. The new family settled into village life, Helen immediately involved herself in village social events and coffee mornings. Helen immediately made friends with her neighbour Margaret Holston, who stated that Helen charmed all the villagers with her parties and welcoming attitude.

Indeed, Helen seemed to bring the neighbourhood closer together. People bonded in a way they had never done before. People in the village suddenly went from being neighbours to becoming friends due to Helen's warm and caring influence. Ian Stewart was a different proposition altogether, people in the village found him "*cold and unfriendly,*" if he didn't just ignore you in the street, the conversation was short and terse and on his terms. Stewart even entered a petty feud with one of his next-door neighbours over a hedge. When the couple's neighbour, Marko Humphrey-Lahti, trimmed the hedge one morning Ian Stewart arrived at Mr Humphrey-Lahti's house shouting and screaming threats and obscenities at Mr Humphrey-Lahti and his wife. Helen Bailey had to drag the enraged and vitriolic Stewart away. Stewart wouldn't let the matter of the hedge go, and a solicitor had to get involved to prove to Stewart that the hedge was Mr Humphrey-Lahti's property to do with as he wanted. Stewart's response to finding out that the hedge belonged to Mr Humphrey-Lahti was to tell the solicitor,

"I don't care what the law says." After this Stewart refused to talk to Mr Humphrey-Lahti and had to be warned about maliciously throwing stones over a fence at Mr Humphrey-Lahti's pet dogs. It was events like this that made many in the village wonder what Helen Bailey actually saw in Ian Stewart. Nevertheless, Helen and Ian became engaged and planned to marry at Brocket Hall country estate. Shortly after moving in together, Ian Stewart took a £1.28 million insurance policy out on Helen's life, and Helen changed her will, unsurprisingly Ian Stewart became her sole beneficiary, if anything were to tragically happen to Helen, Ian Stewart would inherit £4 million.

The first signs of the tragedy began in April 2016. Ian Stewart claimed that Helen had "disappeared" on Monday the 11th of April 2016, but it wasn't until four days later on Friday the 15th of April 2016 that Stewart telephoned the police. Stewart's excuse for not contacting the police sooner was that Helen had left a note saying she needed *"space and time alone... please don't contact me in any way,"* Helen intended to go to their holiday cottage in Broadstairs on the Kent coast. Stewart stated that when he hadn't heard from Helen for a few days, he made enquiries in Broadstairs and discovered that Helen hadn't arrived at her destination. Stewart explained that their relationship had hit a rocky patch, and so he had initially agreed with the sentiments in the letter and had given Helen some space. Rather suspiciously Ian Stewart was unable to show the police the letter allegedly left by Helen, as he claimed he'd thrown it away.

With Helen being a popular and well-known author, her disappearance was immediately front-page news, and the police pulled out all the stops to find her. Chief Inspector Jerome Kent was put in charge of the case, and he had leaflets and posters put up and handed out. Door to door enquiries were made in the little village of Royston and

Broadstairs, and Helen's brother, John Bailey, made a televised appeal for Helen to return home. The police began to search the local area, including the heath that surrounded the village. No sign of Helen could be found anywhere. Friends and neighbours threw themselves into helping the investigation. Her friends and neighbours Margaret Holston and Mavis Drake sent text after text begging Helen to get in touch. Neither one received a reply. Police and Forensic Officers began to try and retrace Helen's last movements, they combed over Hartwell Lodge minutely and read through Helen's diary and private correspondence. Nothing they read indicated that Helen had intended to go off and harm herself, or indeed supported Ian Stewart's story that the relationship had hit a rocky patch. Indeed, Helen's diary seemed to suggest the opposite, she was quite gushing about Stewart and was quite clearly head over heels in love with him. She'd been actively searching the internet for wedding venues just hours before Stewart claimed she'd disappeared. There was something the police found even more interesting. Helen had been complaining of feeling tired and confused all the time and had even mooted that she would probably have to consult her GP about the matter. She'd certainly been worried enough to consult Google about the matter. Could this have had a bearing on her disappearance? Police also removed electronic devices from the property. They examined Helen's electronic footprint. Helen was a big user of social media, she used it to promote and advertise her books and to write her blog, yet she hadn't been on any of her social media sites in days. There was no indication that she was accessing her phone messages or using any of her mobile phone data. More worryingly, she hadn't touched her bank account. Curiously the last transaction had taken place on the morning of Monday the 11th when a standing order to transfer £600 a month into Ian Stewart's bank account had been increased to £4000 a month. Since that transaction, Helen hadn't been near her bank account, so, what was she doing for money?

Helen's electronic footprint ended abruptly at 10:51 a.m. on Monday the 11th of April 2016.

Cliff Lansley and Laura Richards were Behaviour Analysts who examined the initial 999 call that Ian Stewart made to the police. Cliff Lansley counted eight separate occasions were Stewart said *"sorry"* to the operator. In Lansley's considered opinion, this was significant, it showed over-politeness, and therefore was an indicator of deceptive behaviour. Laura Richards felt that it was very significant that Stewart could not answer basic questions about Helen, such as her date of birth or her eye colour. Richards also felt that Stewart having waited four days to telephone the police was a *"red flag"* a worrying anomaly that required urgent further investigation. Richards was also concerned by certain language that Stewart used, specifically that Stewart had said that Helen's phone was "dead." Richards and Lansley both felt that Stewart had disassociated himself from the events of Helen's disappearance. At one point during the 999 call, Stewart was asked when he had last seen Helen. He said that he had gone out, and Helen had stayed at Hartwell Lodge, "*I left her here.*" Stewart said. Cliff Lansley picked up on this curious turn of phrase, "*I left her here,*" as Lansley explained it, "*You might leave an inanimate object, you might leave a dog, you might leave a child or something that's helpless, but why would you leave a grown-up partner there?*" Lansley was of the opinion that it would have been more usual for someone who wasn't trying to dissociate themselves to say "she stayed," at Hartwell Lodge, but Stewart specifically chose to say "*I left her here.*" Subconsciously Stewart had already disassociated himself from Helen to the point where she was now just an object to him, and no longer a person.

Police suspicions were further raised when they discovered that Ian Stewart had attended the offices of solicitor Timothy Penn on Monday the 11th of April

2016, and had asked him to organise the sale of an apartment which Helen Bailey owned in Gateshead. Stewart had informed Mr Penn that Helen was too ill to attend in person but that she wanted the apartment to be placed on the market for £185,000. When Mr Penn stated that he would need to speak to Helen about putting the house up for sale, Ian Stewart adamantly insisted that he had power of attorney and therefore was able to act on Helen's behalf in the matter. Timothy Penn was suspicious and likewise insisted that Helen Bailey should attend the solicitors in person to arrange for the apartments sale.

DCI Kent decided to interview Ian Stewart a second time. At first, Ian Stewart was very reluctant to take part in the interview. Stewart told DCI Kent that he simply *"couldn't be bothered,"* to do the interview, when he realised that the police looked very grimly at this attitude Stewart changed his excuse and told the police he was unwell. The interview finally took place on Thursday the 21st of April 2016 at Hartwell Lodge, this time Detective Constable Hollie Daines video recorded the proceedings. Unfortunately for the police Ian Stewart claimed to have little recollection of the day he'd last seen Helen. He remembered that she'd had an incident while driving to the local shop, which had caused her to be so upset Helen had dramatically declared she was never going to drive again. Stewart also remembered spending a lovely evening watching his son play bowls on the village green. He also remembered going to his local GP to get the bandages changed on some keyhole surgery he'd had. To Cliff Lansley, it was significant that Stewart's amnesia was selective, that he'd had moments of crystal clarity throughout the day, such as his trip to the GP and the bowls match. Certifiable truths that could be proven to have happened. Yet, mixed with the crystal clarity where those hazy moments, almost exclusively linked to his dealings with Helen on the day she disappeared. This indicated to Lansley that Stewart was not being truthful about his dealing with Helen on the day of her disappearance. Stewart was again trying to disassociate himself from Helen and her memory. After the interview, Ian Stewart asked the police if he was still their chief suspect. The police were a little surprised by this question. Although DCI Kent had private suspicions about Stewart, he had never treated him in a manner which would have arisen his suspicions. The investigation was officially a missing person's case, not a murder investigation, officially there were no suspects. So, the police simply placated Stewart by telling him that he was merely a "witness" in the case. This wasn't at all true, DCI Kent suspected foul play, and that Ian Stewart was behind it. Meeting Ian Stewart and interviewing him had only firmed DCI Kent's suspicions, Kent would later say that he felt Ian Stewart was, *"the most bizarre, manipulative, greedy and self-centred man I've ever met."* Based on his suspicions DCI Kent ordered that a secondary search of Hartwell Lodge be carried out. Ian Stewart seemed mightily perturbed by this. He followed

Detective Constable Hollie Daines and Sergeant Nicole Goodyear every step of the way and questioned everything they did and looked at. Behavioural Analyst Laura Richards felt that this behaviour was Stewart trying to assert influence over the investigation and gain possible knowledge of what the police's next move would be.

In June 2016 the police asked if they could carry out a third search of Hartwell Lodge. Ian Stewart refused the request. The police placed Stewart under increased scrutiny, and they found it curious that so soon after Helen's disappearance Stewart had seemingly stopped searching for his fiancé. He had merely gone back to living a life of luxury paid for by Helen Bailey's fortune. Indeed, all of the publicity surrounding Helen's disappearance had an unexpected bonus for the avaricious Stewart. Sales of Helen's books had soared through the roof as her name was pasted all over the papers, the internet and television news. Sales of her book "When Bad Things Happen In Good Bikinis" shot up by 17,000%. The money suddenly came rolling in thick and fast, and Ian Stewart was as happy as Larry about the situation. The first thing he did was buy two season tickets for Arsenal using £4000 from the joint bank account he held with Helen. For the police and the behavioural analysts helping them Ian Stewart's biggest "red flag" was taking himself off on what should have been a romantic two-week holiday to Majorca which had been booked by Helen shortly before her disappearance. This seemed just damn right odd. Why would he put himself through such an experience? Surely, if Stewart was missing Helen, he would spend the whole time he was away mentally torturing himself, imagining what he would have been doing if Helen had been there with him. All the evidence seemed to be pointing in one terrible direction. After careful consideration, the police decided that when he returned for Majorca, they would arrest Ian Stewart for the murder of Helen Bailey. Stewart's response to the arrest was a dismissive, *"You're joking."* The police saw his bluntness and lack of shock as more evidence of his guilt, there were no other protests or declarations of innocence, simply a cocky bravado and a sly grin. Stewart seemed to have a resigned expectation that this had been coming, but that it was no great inconvenience. Stewart asked two rather curious questions of the police upon his arrest, *"Have you found Helen? Is that why the garage door is open?"* At the time the police didn't understand the true significance of these remarks, later they would take on a terrible and chilling significance.

Perhaps Ian Stewart had misplaced confidence that he could wriggle out of the arrest because the police still didn't know where Helen Bailey's body was. This discovery came thanks to a wonderfully nosey neighbour. Mavis Drake was chatting to one of the investigating police officers one day about the conundrum of the missing author and her possible demise. Mavis Drake happened to casually say, *"Well, you know about the well, of course."* No, the police didn't know anything about any well. What Mavis Drake was euphemistically talking about was a cesspit hidden underneath the garage at Hartwell Lodge. The police trudged back to Hartwell Lodge and found the cesspit. They hadn't previously noticed it as Helen Bailey's Jeep had been moved from its usual spot in the driveway into the garage where for months it had hidden the cesspit from the eyes of the investigating officers. The police moved the jeep, opened the cesspit up and there lying in the filth and feculence was the rotting corpse of Helen Bailey and her beloved dachshund, Boris. Pathologist Dr Nathanial Carey examined Helen's body, he found that there was no sign of a struggle or any violence, but toxicologist Dr Mark Piper discovered that Helen's system was stuffed to the gills with Zopiclone, a sleeping drug which Ian Stewart had been prescribed by his GP. The police finally had all the evidence they needed to charge Ian Stewart with Helen Bailey's murder.

Ian Stewart's trial for the murder of Helen Bailey began at St Alban's Crown Court on Tuesday the 10th of January 2017, before Mr Justice Andrew Bright QC. Stewart Trimmer QC headed the prosecution and stated that Ian Stewart had played a *"long game"* when plotting to murder Helen Bailey and that his involvement in the missing person enquiry had been *"a cynical, deceitful and calculated charade."* The prosecution believed that Ian Stewart wanted Helen Bailey to believe she had been losing her mind. By administering the sleeping drug Zopiclone Stewart had made Helen woozy and disorientated, and caused her to have problems with her short term memory, she'd even forgotten how to type. Stewart had hoped that with these chemically induced neurological problems he would be able to get power of attorney over Helen and therefore full control of her money. When his plan didn't work, and Helen began to realise she may be being drugged, Ian Stewart had waited until Helen fell asleep on the settee one day and then suffocated her with a pillow. Stewart had then dumped Helen's body in the cesspit and took the pillow and mattress to the local dump.

Simon Russell Flint QC for the defence argued that Ian Stewart had no need to try and get control of Helen's fortune as he was more cash-rich than Helen. Although this was not the main thrust of Ian Stewart's defence, which was something a heck of a lot more ludicrous. Stewart put forward the ridiculous story that Helen had been kidnapped by two former business associates of John Sinfield's called Nick and Joe. These men stated that Helen was coming with them to *"Help solve a problem."* The dastardly Nick and Joe had threatened Ian Stewart, physically punching him, and told him that if he went to the police not only would Helen die, so too would his two sons. Stewart had no idea what the problem was that Nick and Joe had, or how they hoped Helen would be able to solve it. Nick and Joe had also demanded £500,000 for the safe return of Helen, and that was why Stewart had been so desperate to put Helen's flat up for sale. Reading the accounts of the trial were two men who recognised the description of Nick and Joe. These men were Ian Stewart's former neighbours from the village of Bassingbourn, Nick Cook and Joe Cippullo. Fearing that Ian Stewart was trying to set them up for Helen's murder they both went straight around to the police and told them their fears, and also their cast iron alibis for the day of the murder. The police passed Mr Cook and Mr Cippullo onto the Crown Prosecution Services who had both men brought to St Alban's Crown Court. Here the jury could quite clearly see that Ian Stewart had based his fictitious kidnappers on his wholly innocent former neighbours. Stewart Trimmer QC summed up Ian Stewart's defence as being *"bizarre nonsense... quite absurd."* With the defence pretty much in tatters, Defence barrister Simon Russell Flint QC was left desperately sniping and picking tiny holes in the prosecution's case. They traipsed witness after witness into the court to testify that they had seen Helen after the time the prosecution insisted she should have been dead. The inference being that if the prosecution couldn't get the time of Helen's death right, could the jury be certain of anything else the prosecution claimed. Simon Russell Flint QC stated that the prosecution had nothing more to offer than, *"highly speculative theories,"* and asked the jury the simple question, *"What possible motive could (Stuart) have? What caused this mild-mannered, loving family man... what made him suddenly decide to kill Helen Bailey? It makes no sense at all. It's complete nonsense. It's rubbish."*

On Wednesday the 22nd of February 2017, the jury retired to consider its verdict. It took them six hours to come to a consensus, they eventually returned with a Guilty verdict. The case was adjourned for Pre-Sentence Reports to be compiled by the National Probation Service. On the day of sentence, Ian Stewart was due to appear in court via a video-link. Stewart refused to leave his cell to hear Simon Russell Flint QC mitigate on his behalf, or Mr Justice Bright QC to pronounce the sentence. Nevertheless, Mr Justice Bright QC proceeded to sentence as if Ian Stewart were present, and stated that it was, *"difficult to imagine a more heinous crime,"* and that Stewart had spun a, *"calculated and callous series of lies...wicked lies."* The learned judge went on to pour scorn over Ian Stewart and his horrid machinations, *"You knew Helen Bailey to be a wealthy woman but were not content with having to share in her wealth as her husband. Instead, you wanted it all for yourself... I am firmly of the view that you currently pose a real danger to women with whom you form a relationship."* Mr Justice Bright sentenced Ian Stewart to thirty-four years imprisonment. Simon Russell Flint QC stated after the trial that this is effectively a whole life tariff for Ian Stewart, as he will be ninety-years-old before he is eligible for parole.

Conclusion

What have we learnt from these bloody stories? Well, if you're going to have an affair, make sure you do so discreetly. Don't have public disagreements with your husband and or lover. If your lover decides they want to off an inconvenient spouse, do your best to persuade them otherwise, or you might find yourself stood beside them in the dock. If your relationship hits problems, be them general boredom, or the more serious issue of spousal abuse, seek help as quickly as you can, you may be able to save the relationship if it's only boredom that bothers you, or indeed, save your own life if the relationship is turning violent. Most of all, being with someone, being in love, is meant to make us happy, not miserable, or scared or frightened. If you find that one day it's stopped being fun, then it might be best to stop doing it. Cherish the happy memories, and walk away before you have too many bad ones, or the allure of a more permanent and murderous end to your misery just might become an attractive option.

Happy Valentine's.

Selected Bibliography

As I have always stated in the bibliographies for the Murder Tales series, if you enjoyed reading the chilling tales of murder I have recounted on these pages then there are lots of other books and websites out there which feature accounts of these crimes, some of which helped in the research of Murder Tales: Love You To Death. Below is a none exhaustive list of just some of those books available:

Beyond Bad: Sandra Lee – Bantam Books – 2002

Blood Stain: Peter Lalor – Allen & Unwin - 2002

Deadly Innocence: Scott Burnside and Alan Cairns – Warner Books – 1995

Domestic Poisoners: Martin Fido – Apple - 2009

Invisible Darkness: Stephen Williams – Bantam – 2002

The Mammoth Book of Bizarre Crimes: Robin Odell - Robinson - 2010

The Murder Book of Days: Brian Lane - Headline – 1995

Murder Guide To London: Martin Fido – Harper Collins - 1987

Murderous Manchester, The Executed of the Twentieth Century: John D. Eddleston – Derby Books Publishing – 2011

www.bbc.co.uk/news

www.truecrimelibrary.com

www.trutv.com

www.youtube.com

Enjoy this book? You can make a big difference!

Reviews are the most important thing in getting my books noticed by other readers. If you enjoyed reading this book, you could make a huge difference by spending just five minutes leaving a review on the Amazon page.

Thank you.

You can purchase other titles in the Murder Tales series here:

UK:
https://www.amazon.co.uk/s?k=Murder+Tales+H.+N.+Lloyd&ref=nb_sb_noss_2

US:
https://www.amazon.com/s?k=Murder+Tales+H.+N.+Lloyd&ref=nb_sb_noss_2

Other titles available in the Murder Tales series:

Murder Tales: Unsolved

Murder Tales: The Christmas Companion

Murder Tales: The Granny Killers

Murder Tales: The Valentine Companion

Murder Tales: They Got Away With Murder

Murder Tales: The Mummy's Boys

Murder Tales: Fatal Fame

Murder Tales: The Lesbian Vampire Killers

---

[i] Alice hadn't helped matters by lying to the police and initially telling them that she was Wainwrights wife.

[ii] After three days the police realised that Alice Day had simply been in the wrong place at the wrong time and let her go free of charge.

[iii] Dr De Kaplany fled Hungary via the United Kingdom, it is also suggested that it was only upon his arrival in England that he added the prefix "De" to the name Kaplany.

[iv] Anderson believed Jane Hajdu had ulterior motives for trying to break-up the marriage, that Jane Hajdu probably fancied De Kaplany herself and with Hajna out of the way believed she could make a play for the arrogant anaesthetist

v *This is the Australian equivalent of a Restraining Order or a Domestic Violence Prevention Order.*

vi *Katherine Knight made two $500 transactions within the space of two minutes. Price's card had a limit of $500 per transaction.*

vii *The police investigated the allegation of rape and child abuse that Katherine Knight put in her suicide note and found them to be absolutely groundless.*

[viii] Hertfordshire Police have stated that they are now investigating the circumstances of Diane Stewart's death to see if Ian Stewart had any part in her demise. They may find this difficult, seeing at Ian Stewart had Diane's body cremated as soon as the coroner released it back to the family.

Printed in Great Britain
by Amazon

76127652R00177